The Runner's Training Diary For Dummies®

FOR DUMMIES™ BESTSELLING BOOK SERIES

Cheat Sheet

Sample Diary

Training Goals
Goals!

T0114136

Prepare for town 10K on 5/7

Work toward marathon — 10/18

Date: 4/2

Training	Time/Distance	Sets	Reps
LSD run	28 min/3 miles		

Food for Thought
felt great! Bringing walkman really helped

Date: 4/3

Training	Time/Distance	Sets	Reps
Intervals			
Warmup	6 min/1 ½ miles		
2 short sprints	25 yards		
2 medium sprints	100 yards		

Food for Thought
Remember to keep stride rate high

For Dummies™: Bestselling Book Series for Beginners

The Runner's Training Diary For Dummies®

Cheat Sheet

Personal Running Bests

Long, steady distance (LSD)	Time/Date	Time/Date	Time/Date
1 mile			
2 miles			
5K (3.1 miles)			
10K (6.2 miles)			
Half marathon			

Sprints	Time/Date	Time/Date	Time/Date
20 yards			
50 yards			
100 yards			
200 yards			

Race pace	Time/Date	Time/Date	Time/Date
1 mile			
2 miles			
5K (3.1 miles)			
10K (6.2 miles)			

Race Day Checklist

- ❑ Sweats
- ❑ Sunglasses
- ❑ Hat
- ❑ Sunscreen
- ❑ Watch
- ❑ Heart-rate monitor
- ❑ Safety pins (for your number)
- ❑ Money
- ❑ Change
- ❑ Identification
- ❑ Change of clothes
- ❑ Change of shoes

The Wiley logo is a registered trademark under exclusive license to Wiley Publishing, Inc., from International Data Group, Inc. The ...For Dummies logo and For Dummies are trademarks of Wiley Publishing, Inc. All other trademarks are the property of their respective owners.

WILEY

For Dummies™: Bestselling Book Series for Beginners

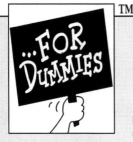 TM

References for the Rest of Us ™

BESTSELLING BOOK SERIES

Do you find that traditional reference books are overloaded with technical details and advice you'll never use? Do you postpone important life decisions because you just don't want to deal with them? Then our *...For Dummies*® business and general reference book series is for you.

...For Dummies business and general reference books are written for those frustrated and hard-working souls who know they aren't dumb, but find that the myriad of personal and business issues and the accompanying horror stories make them feel helpless. *...For Dummies* books use a lighthearted approach, a down-to-earth style, and even cartoons and humorous icons to dispel fears and build confidence. Lighthearted but not lightweight, these books are perfect survival guides to solve your everyday personal and business problems.

Already, millions of satisfied readers agree. They have made *...For Dummies* the #1 introductory level computer book series and a best-selling business book series. They have written asking for more. So, if you're looking for the best and easiest way to learn about business and other general reference topics, look to *...For Dummies* to give you a helping hand.

IDG
BOOKS
WORLDWIDE

1/99

The Runner's Training Diary FOR DUMMIES®

by Allen St. John

IDG Books Worldwide, Inc.
An International Data Group Company

Foster City, CA ✦ Chicago, IL ✦ Indianapolis, IN ✦ New York, NY

The Runner's Training Diary For Dummies

Published by

IDG Books Worldwide, Inc.

An International Data Group Company

919 E, Hillsdale Blvd.

Suite 300

Foster City, CA 94404

www.idgbooks.com (IDG Books Worldwide Web site)

www.dummies.com (Dummies Press Web site)

Library of Congress Control Number: 00-111274

ISBN: 0-7645-5338-0

10 9 8 7 6 5 4 3 2 1

1O/QX/QS/QR/IN

Distributed in the United States by IDG Books Worldwide, Inc.

Distributed by CDG Books Canada Inc. for Canada; by Transworld Publishers Limited in the United Kingdom; by IDG Norge Books for Norway; by IDG Sweden Books for Sweden; by IDG Books Australia Publishing Corporation Pty. Ltd. for Australia and New Zealand; by TransQuest Publishers Pte Ltd. for Singapore, Malaysia, Thailand, Indonesia, and Hong Kong; by Gotop Information Inc. for Taiwan; by ICG Muse, Inc. for Japan; by Intersoft for South Africa; by Eyrolles for France; by International Thomson Publishing for Germany, Austria and Switzerland; by Distribuidora Cuspide for Argentina; by LR International for Brazil; by Galileo Libros for Chile; by Ediciones ZETA S.C.R. Ltda. for Peru; by WS Computer Publishing Corporation, Inc., for the Philippines; by Contemporanea de Ediciones for Venezuela; by Express Computer Distributors for the Caribbean and West Indies; by Micronesia Media Distributor, Inc. for Micronesia; by Chips Computadoras S.A. de C.V. for Mexico; by Editorial Norma de Panama S.A. for Panama; by American Bookshops for Finland.

For general information on IDG Books Worldwide's books in the U.S., please call our Consumer Customer Service department at 800-762-2974. For reseller information, including discounts and premium sales, please call our Reseller Customer Service department at 800-434-3422.

For information on where to purchase IDG Books Worldwide's books outside the U.S., please contact our International Sales department at 317-572-3993 or fax 317-572-4002.

For consumer information on foreign language translations, please contact our Customer Service department at 1-800-434-3422, fax 317-572-4002, or e-mail rights@idgbooks.com.

For information on licensing foreign or domestic rights, please phone +1-650-653-7098.

For sales inquiries and special prices for bulk quantities, please contact our Order Services department at 800-434-4322 or write to the address above.

For information on using IDG Books Worldwide's books in the classroom or for ordering examination copies, please contact our Educational Sales department at 800-434-2086 or fax 317-572-4005.

For press review copies, author interviews, or other publicity information, please contact our Public Relations department at 650-653-7000 or fax 650-653-7500.

For authorization to photocopy items for corporate, personal, or educational use, please contact Copyright Clearance Center, 222 Rosewood Drive, Danvers, MA 01923, or fax 978-750-4470.

is a registered trademark under exclusive license to IDG Books Worldwide, Inc., from International Data Group, Inc.

About the Author

Allen St. John is the author of *Bicycling For Dummies* and *Skiing For Dummies* and is a former senior editor at *Condé Nast Women's Sports and Fitness* magazine. An avid recreational athlete, he has written about sports and fitness for a wide variety of national newspapers and magazines including *Men's Journal, MH-18, U.S. News & World Report, Maxim,* and the *New York Times.* He's a columnist for *Skiing* magazine, a regular contributor to *Tennis,* and a founding contributing editor for *Bike,* and he has covered the New York Yankees for the *Village Voice* for the past eight seasons, as well as contributed to the hardcover book and CD-ROM, *The Way Baseball Works.* He lives in Upper Montclair, New Jersey, with his wife, Sally, and two children, Ethan and Emma.

ABOUT IDG BOOKS WORLDWIDE

Welcome to the world of IDG Books Worldwide.

IDG Books Worldwide, Inc., is a subsidiary of International Data Group, the world's largest publisher of computer-related information and the leading global provider of information services on information technology. IDG was founded more than 30 years ago by Patrick J. McGovern and now employs more than 9,000 people worldwide. IDG publishes more than 290 computer publications in over 75 countries. More than 90 million people read one or more IDG publications each month.

Launched in 1990, IDG Books Worldwide is today the #1 publisher of best-selling computer books in the United States. We are proud to have received eight awards from the Computer Press Association in recognition of editorial excellence and three from Computer Currents' First Annual Readers' Choice Awards. Our best-selling ...For Dummies® series has more than 50 million copies in print with translations in 31 languages. IDG Books Worldwide, through a joint venture with IDG's Hi-Tech Beijing, became the first U.S. publisher to publish a computer book in the People's Republic of China. In record time, IDG Books Worldwide has become the first choice for millions of readers around the world who want to learn how to better manage their businesses.

Our mission is simple: Every one of our books is designed to bring extra value and skill-building instructions to the reader. Our books are written by experts who understand and care about our readers. The knowledge base of our editorial staff comes from years of experience in publishing, education, and journalism — experience we use to produce books to carry us into the new millennium. In short, we care about books, so we attract the best people. We devote special attention to details such as audience, interior design, use of icons, and illustrations. And because we use an efficient process of authoring, editing, and desktop publishing our books electronically, we can spend more time ensuring superior content and less time on the technicalities of making books.

You can count on our commitment to deliver high-quality books at competitive prices on topics you want to read about. At IDG Books Worldwide, we continue in the IDG tradition of delivering quality for more than 30 years. You'll find no better book on a subject than one from IDG Books Worldwide.

John Kilcullen
Chairman and CEO
IDG Books Worldwide, Inc.

Eighth Annual Computer Press Awards ≥1992

Ninth Annual Computer Press Awards ≥1993

Tenth Annual Computer Press Awards ≥1994

Eleventh Annual Computer Press Awards ≥1995

Dedication

To my kids, Ethan and Emma, who do everything they can to keep me in shape.

Author's Acknowledgments

Although there's one name on the cover, a book is a team effort. I'd like to thank everyone at IDG Books, including executive editor Stacy Collins and project editors Mike Kelly and Greg Summers, and of course my agent, the incomparable Mark Reiter, and the rest of the good people at IMG Literary. Special thanks go to this book's technical reviewer, Jeff Csatari, who helped make sure that the information in this book is as smart and accurate as it can be.

Thanks also to all the editors who help me make a living putting words together, including James Kaminsky, Albert Baime, and Alex Straus at *Maxim,* David Sparrow, James Martin, and Bill Gray at *Tennis,* Rick Kahl, Helen Olsson, Bevin Wallace, Mike Miracle, and Charlie Glass at *Skiing,* Dana White at *Teen People,* Brian Duffy at *U.S. News & World Report,* King Kaufman at *Salon.com,* Jerry Beilinson at *National Geographic Adventure,* Miles Seligman at the *Village Voice,* Michael Anderson at the *New York Times Book Review,* Jack Schwartz at the *New York Times,* Kyle Creighton at the *New York Times Magazine,* and, of course, anyone that I'm forgetting.

And finally to my wife, Sally, my support, my inspiration, and my best friend.

Publisher's Acknowledgments

We're proud of this book; please send us your comments through our IDG Books Worldwide Online Registration Form located at www.dummies.com.

Some of the people who helped bring this book to market include the following:

Acquisitions, Editorial, and Media Development

Project Editors: Michael Kelly, Greg Summers

Executive Editor: Stacy S. Collins

Copy Editor: Robert Annis

Acquisitions Coordinator: Stacy Klein

General Reviewer: Jeff Csatari

Editorial Manager: Jennifer Ehrlich

Editorial Administrator: Michelle Hacker

Cover Photos:
Front Cover John Henley/TSM
Back Cover Michael Pole/Corbis

Production

Project Coordinator: Dale White

Layout and Graphics: Amy Adrian, Sean Decker, LeAndra Johnson, Brian Torwelle, Julie Trippetti

Special Art:

Proofreaders: Andy Hollandbeck, Susan Moritz, Carl Pierce, Nancy Price, Marianne Santy, York Production Services, Inc.

Indexer: York Production Services, Inc.

General and Administrative

IDG Books Worldwide, Inc.: John Kilcullen, CEO; Bill Barry, President and COO; John Ball, Executive VP, Operations & Administration; John Harris, CFO

IDG Books Consumer Reference Group

Business: Kathleen A. Welton, Vice President and Publisher; Kevin Thornton, Acquisitions Manager

Cooking/Gardening: Jennifer Feldman, Associate Vice President and Publisher

Education/Reference: Diane Graves Steele, Vice President and Publisher; Greg Tubach, Publishing Director

Lifestyles: Kathleen Nebenhaus, Vice President and Publisher; Tracy Boggier, Managing Editor

Pets: Dominique De Vito, Associate Vice President and Publisher; Tracy Boggier, Managing Editor

Travel: Michael Spring, Vice President and Publisher; Suzanne Jannetta, Editorial Director; Brice Gosnell, Managing Editor

IDG Books Consumer Editorial Services: Kathleen Nebenhaus, Vice President and Publisher; Kristin A. Cocks, Editorial Director; Cindy Kitchel, Editorial Director

IDG Books Consumer Production: Debbie Stailey, Production Director

IDG Books Packaging: Marc J. Mikulich, Vice President, Brand Strategy and Research

◆

The publisher would like to give special thanks to Patrick J. McGovern, without whom this book would not have been possible.

◆

Contents at a Glance

Cartoons at a Glance

By Rich Tennant

"This readout shows your heart rate, blood pressure, bone density, skin hydration, plaque buildup, liver function, and expected lifetime."

page 57

"You know, anyone who wishes he had a remote control for his exercise equipment is missing the idea of exercise equipment."

page 181

"I'm not sure I can live up to my workout clothes."

page 7

Cartoon Information:
Fax: 978-546-7747
E-Mail: richtennant@the5thwave.com
World Wide Web: www.the5thwave.com

Table of Contents

Introduction

There's something very simple and almost magical about running. You put one foot in front of the other, and before long, you've got a couple of miles under your belt. And tomorrow, you find that today's sweat pays dividends. You discover that you can run farther and faster than you did last week. This book is about helping you toward those oh-wow moments when you find yourself able to do something that you never could before.

About This Book

So you've decided to hide that bowl of nacho chips, pop the AAA batteries out of the remote, and get off the couch for good. Congratulations. But while that first step is important, the real key to getting in shape — and staying there — is consistency. Day after day, week after week, month after month, you need to make exercise as much a part of your day as brushing your teeth. And that's where this book comes in.

Part information source, part motivational tool, and part journal, this book will help you get started exercising, help you to get the most out of every workout, and, yes, even supply a gentle kick in the pants when your willpower flags. Not bad for a pile of paper that fits in your gym bag.

In these pages, you find out how to set up an exercise program that's just right for you. You discover how to warm up properly to prevent injuries. You get a wealth of workout tips in a variety of popular workout activities, from walking to swimming to in-line skating. Finally, you find out about how to cool down and recharge for your next workout.

And then comes the part of the book that you write yourself. The meat of this book is a customizable workout log where you can list your personal goals and record your progress. It's this section that makes this book truly *your* book.

And finally, because everyone loves a list, the Part of Tens, which gives you a few more tips and even a couple of jokes.

Why You Should Log Your Workouts

First, here's what you shouldn't expect from this book. It won't improve your penmanship. It won't win you a Pulitzer Prize. And unless you win, say, a Nobel Prize or a presidential election on your own, it won't provide an insight into your personality for biographers of a future generation.

What logging your workouts does give you is pretty simple: motivation and information. First the motivation part. Have you ever made a to-do list? Have you ever made a to-do list after you've already completed the first three tasks, just so you get the satisfaction of crossing them off? Admit it, it's a great feeling. That's the same kind of reward that's waiting for you at the end of every exercise session.

The great thing about fitness is that it's quantifiable. Practice your new arrangement of "Afternoon Delight" on your Casiotone for a month, and you're depending on your friends to tell you how much better you sound. But when it comes to fitness, you're not dependent on the kindness of strangers. All you need to do is flip back through your training diary and realize that you're going farther and faster, or lifting more, than you did a month ago. Trust me, that's also a great feeling.

But unlike your old to-do lists, the completed pages of this training diary will also contain plenty of vital information. You'll see which goals were easy and fun to attain, and which goals made you feel like Wile E. Coyote chasing the Road Runner. By reviewing your entries, you'll be able to detect personal patterns and tendencies that will allow you to train more efficiently in the future. You'll also be able to improve your performance and prevent injuries. And, finally, you'll be able to have more fun . . . beyond the simple joy of seeing your accomplishments immortalized in black and white.

How to Use Your Training Diary

The first thing you need to use your training diary is a pen.
Got it? Good. The next thing you need is a plan. Before you
start keeping a training diary, you should have a basic idea
of what your fitness goals are and how to achieve them.
(Don't worry, I talk about all that in Chapter 1.)

The next thing you need is a willingness to make your training diary your new friend. Bring this book with you to the
gym, keeping it in your gym bag right next to your shower
shoes. Or if you exercise outdoors, set it down on the
kitchen counter, right next to a bottle of Gatorade, and make
a beeline for it as soon as you get back from an exercise session. As soon as you've completed a workout, make it a habit
to write down what you did and how you felt. If you record
your workout right away, it's easy and fun. If you wait until
later, it becomes a hassle. Or doesn't get done at all.

At the minimum, you should record how long you worked
out, how many reps at each weight you did in the weight
room, or the duration and distance of your aerobic workout.
You might also record how you felt when you got up and
before, during, and after your workout.

Because I know you're busy, this diary doesn't assume that
you're going to work out every day of every week — in fact,
a good workout plan includes a healthy balance of exercise
and rest. With the diary section, you can track your progress
over a ten-day stretch, customizing your journal each day for
whatever workout you choose, running, weight training, and
so on. And you can use the Training Goals section to write
down your personal training goals and the Workout Wrap-Up
section to celebrate your training accomplishments.

Finally, don't forget the Food for Thought section to track
your diet and nutrition goals, as well as how you felt during
your workout and what you should focus on for your next
training session.

But this isn't a police report — your training diary can
include anything that you feel is important. Did "99
Luftbaloons" keep running through your head on your bike
ride? Did you finally figure out in mid-rep why Ginger

brought all those dresses for a three-hour tour? Did you step on the scale after your shower and finally see the needle settle at your target weight? Then write it down.

Cheater, Cheater, Biscotti Eater

"When you cheat, you're only cheating yourself." Bet you haven't heard that one since grammar school. Well, I'm hear to tell you that Mrs. Moloney was right — about that, not about the fact that you'll never amount to anything unless you sit up straighter at your desk.

So while it's very tempting to write in on that first line — ran 7 miles / 42 minutes or bench press: 225 pounds — don't do it unless you really did it. First off, remember that this is a diary. And like the one with the poodle fur and the tiny gold key in which you promised your undying love to Jimmy Whatshisname, it's completely private. Your little sister won't read it unless you show it to her, so there's no need to hide it under the bed. Unless you decide to share it with your friends — or leave it for your biographer — no one's going to be impressed by what you wrote down, or think less of you if your workout was kind of lame.

So if you don't complete your planned workout on any given day, that's okay. Write down what you did and, if you can, why you think you fell short of your goal. Too tired? Too sore? Too little time? That info will help you down the road.

If you skip a couple of days of working out, that's okay, too. But if you start fudging and writing down miles not run and weights not lifted, you won't have an accurate yardstick of what you really did and how fast you really progressed. When you go back a couple of months later, you'll feel like a special prosecutor, trying to piece together who did what when. So take some sage advice from Samuel Langhorne Clemens — "When in doubt, tell the truth." Somewhere down the road, you'll be glad you did.

How This Book Is Organized

Okay, this isn't *Anna Karenina* and I don't expect you to sit down with a bottle of vodka and a box of tissues and read it from start to finish. But this book does have a beginning, middle, and end. First off, you get a bit of sage advice. In the opening chapters, you'll find out how this book is organized — in fact that's what you're doing right now — how to plan a workout program, how to warm up properly, how to get the most out of your workout, and how to cool down and refuel for your next workout.

After that comes the place where you take center stage: the training diary pages. These pages will give you a place to make a workout plan that's customized for your level of fitness, your goals, and your schedule. You'll also have a place to record each workout and monitor your progress. Each spread is complete with a fitness factoid or a quote guaranteed to pique your curiosity.

The book closes with the Part of Tens, a couple of short chapters filled with a few more amusing tips. And finally, the index will help you locate anything you can't find on your own.

Icons Used in This Book

As with any *For Dummies* book, this one has icons to act as guideposts to special hints and notions along the way, each one offering a helpful perspective to consider as you plan your workout.

This icon highlights a quick hint that will help you train better and more efficiently.

Items flagged with this icon will help you to avoid accidents and injuries.

This icon is the graphic equivalent of a string tied around your finger, a reminder about something that you can't — or shouldn't — do without during your training or your race.

This icon flags training technique suggestions, workout gear recommendations, and fun facts you can use to amaze your friends at cocktail parties.

Information included with this icon offer suggestions that will make your workouts easier.

Where to Go from Here

The important thing about training is to get started *today*. And start tracking your progress *today*. The sooner you start to make use of this book's diary and log your workout progress, the sooner you can see improvements in your daily training regimen. So turn the page (or use the Table of Contents or Index to get to the information you need the most) and get going!

Part I
The Training Basics

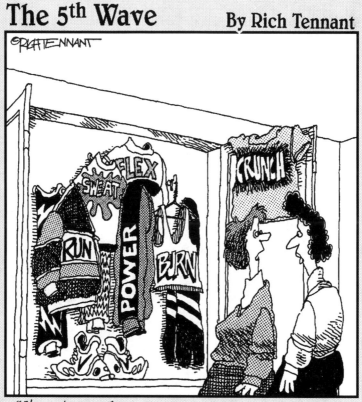

"I'm not sure I can live up to my workout clothes."

In this part . . .

Ready to go? Good. But before you lace up your sneakers, pour yourself a cup of coffee, sit down, and spend a few minutes reading this section, where you'll learn how to get ready for a workout, train as efficiently as possible, and get ready for next time.

Chapter 1

Creating Your Workout Plan

*W*hat do you have in common with a world-class athlete and a James Bond supervillain? Each of you
needs a plan. The good news is that you don't need to draw
blood three times a day to check your lactate levels, and you
don't need an evil laugh and a world map marking every
missle silo to . . . *Ha Ha Hmmm . . . Rule the World!*

Even if you're not after a gold medal or global domination,
but you simply want to lose a few pounds, a plan helps in
any number of ways. It makes your workouts more efficient
and helps you to see results more quickly.

Conversely, if you start a workout program without a plan,
you're like that classic Sex Pistols song — don't know what
you want, but you know how to get it.

Why Exercise Anyway?

Before you delve into the whats, wheres, and hows of
creating your own exercise program, back up and think
about *why* you exercise in the first place. You probably
know a lot of the answers, but listing them may just be the

difference between getting up for that 6:30 workout or hitting the snooze button.

- **You'll be healthier:** By exercising, you can reduce your risk of serious and even life-threatening diseases such as diabetes, heart disease, and cancer. There's even evidence that exercise can ward off the common cold.

- **You'll look better:** Exercising not only burns calories but also boosts your metabolism, which makes it easier to maintain your desired weight without resorting to the celery and ice cream diet.

- **You'll be less stressed:** Exercise produces endorphins — the same mood-altering brain chemicals that are targeted by everything from chocolate to illicit drugs. Runner's high is more than a myth.

- **You'll have fun:** Remember when you used to go out and play after school, running and jumping, riding and skating until you were exhausted? Well, pick the right exercise and that same kind of fun is still there for the taking.

Making Your Fitness Plan

If the road to fitness is a journey, then a fitness plan is your road map. You don't need to be a motivational guru to understand that before you can get in shape, you've got to identify some workout goals and figure out how to get from here to there.

First, you've got to identify your destination, or your goal. In this section, I tell you how to do that. Once you know where you're going, it becomes a lot easier to map out the shortest route there, which I discuss later in this chapter.

Setting your fitness goals

In workouts and in life, goal setting can be both easy and hard. At its most basic level, setting a goal is as simple as identifying something you want. It can be as vague as, "I want to be happy." Or as specific as, "I want to be the executive vice president in charge of marketing by the end of September."

Workout-wise, you've got the same range of choices. Your objective can be as general as wanting to be healthier and feel better and have some fun. Or it can be as specific as saying, "I want to break 50 minutes in the Independence Day 10K." Or, "I want to drop 12 pounds and 2 dress sizes so that I'm looking good for Chris's wedding in August."

The bottom line is that the quality of the goal you set is directly proportional to your chance of achieving it. If your goal is too vague, it can be almost impossible to measure your progress. ("Do I really feel healthier and feel better than I did last week?")

If the goal is too specific, that can be a problem too. If you become too goal-oriented — "I've been exercising for three weeks and my time (or waistline) hasn't come down at all." — it's easy to get discouraged by slow progress or minor setbacks.

The best goals are those that have both macro and micro components. Your macro goal might be, "I want to run the New York City Marathon next year." Your micro goal might be, "I want to run the 5K in town faster than I did last year." In short, your everyday goal should be an easily achievable, bite-size chunk of that larger goal. The short-term goal gives you a reason to work out today — "The 5K is ten days away" is a much better incentive for getting out of bed than, say, "The marathon is ten months away."

And once you achieve that micro goal, you can pat yourself on the back, because you did what you set out to do, and you've also moved a little closer to your big objective. Which makes it easier to set another micro goal.

Finding the time

The world's number-one all-purpose excuse? *I'm too busy.* Do you know anyone who's *not* too busy? I even hear it from my three-year-old son Ethan when I ask him to pick up his trains. "But, Daddy, I'm too busy." So let's find a way past the "B" word, shall we?

The first step is to make exercise a priority. Whether we write things down or not, every day each of us has a giant to-do list — with standing entries ranging from taking a shower

More than the standard disclaimer

My lawyers want me to tell you that you should consult your physician before beginning a program of physical exercise. Okay, there I said it. But I'd like this to sink in more than the seat-belt demonstration on an airliner. After all, you wouldn't take a car that's been in storage for five years straight to the drag strip, now would you?

Well, if your car deserves a trip to the mechanic, don't you deserve a trip to your friendly neighborhood physician? A pre-exercise physical exam can uncover some underlying problems — anything from heart disease to a blood sugar imbalance — that could be exacerbated by exercise. So do the right thing — go see your doctor.

to making enough money to pay the mortgage. So what you need to do is add one more thing that you absolutely, positively must do today: Get some exercise.

The best way to make sure that exercise becomes as automatic as brushing your teeth? Make it part of your schedule. Here are a few ways to incorporate exercise into your daily routine.

✔ **Do it early:** You remember Murphy's Law, right? Well, one of its axioms is that if you put off your workout until after work, and you go to the DMV, do grocery shopping, and drop the kids off at their friends' house, the following will happen. The DMV line will snake around the block, the baggers at the grocery store will stage a sitdown strike, and you'll get caught in a traffic jam on the way to the play date. In short, everything that can go wrong, will, and you'll be running an hour late, and today's workout will have to wait until tomorrow. If you work out first thing in the morning, you won't have to worry about life's little intrusions.

✔ **Multi-task:** Exercising can be tacked on to other chores, if you make it the first task, rather than the last. Stopping at the gym on your way to work, or right after you drop the kids off at school, is a great way to make sure that it gets done.

✔ **Get help:** Familes and friends can place demands on you that can keep you from exercising. Or they can help clear your schedule so that you have the time. If you're having trouble finding time to exercise, talk to the people in your life. Whether it's trading chores to get a big enough block of time to go to the gym, or just asking for a little good-natured nagging — "So, lard butt, have you gone running yet or what?" — your significant others can lend a hand in helping you get into shape.

Setting Up Your Workout Schedule

Now that you've identified some goals and carved out some time to exercise, the next step is to make a workout plan. Some of the benefits of having a workout plan are obvious.

If you've made a plan in advance, it eliminates what coaches call "game-time decision-making." It allows you to glance at the day's schedule and go out and do it, rather than trying to remember what your last workout was, and whether tomorrow's a rest day or not. Which means that you get out of the house and start breaking a sweat sooner.

But the biggest difference between having a workout plan and just going out and exercising is this: When you create a plan, you balance rest and recovery, and every workout has a specific purpose in helping you achieve your fitness goals. It's really about squeezing the maximum fitness benefit out of the minimum amount of time.

Build a smart plan and stick to it, and I guarantee you'll be stronger, fitter, and faster. And if after a month or two you can suddenly fit into a pair of jeans that you thought were two sizes too small, well, so much the better.

The first thing you need to do is determine how many days a week you're going to be working out. If you're just starting out, three is a good number. And it's best to balance workout days with rest and recovery days (see Chapter 4 for more about the importance of rest). For that reason, you might start out by working out on Monday, Wednesday, and Friday. Or Tuesday, Thursday, and Saturday if that suits you better.

And if you're doing cross-training — combining two or more activities in your workout plan — then it makes sense to alternate your activities in addition to your workouts. For example, if you're going to ride your bike twice a week, swim once a week, and do one weight training session, your schedule might shake out like the one in Table 1-1.

Table 1-1   A Typical Cross-Training Workout Schedule

Sun	Mon	Tue	Wed	Thu	Fri	Sat
Rest	30 min Bike	Rest	30 min Swim + Resistance training	Rest	40 min Bike	Rest

The specifics aren't as important as the general principles. In Table 1-1, I've alternated the rest and exercise days. The two bike rides are separated by two and three days, respectively, to give you ample time to recover. The duration of the workouts increases gradually through the week. And since you're going to the health club to swim, that's a good day to put in a few minutes in the weight room.

Of course, you can feel free to modify this plan to fit your schedule, your level of fitness, and your goals.

What about next week? In general, it's good to keep your weekly schedule pretty much the same from week to week. Schedule with the longer workouts and gym sessions on the same day, if possible. And while you should add to the length of the workouts, as your fitness level allows, don't push it too hard. Adding more than 10 percent a week is only inviting injury.

Getting into Training

So you've already been doing this exercise thing for a while? Well, congratulations. Now may be the time for you to move from the land of the unstructured workout into full-fledged training.

Training? Don't get freaked out by the "T" word. Yeah, that's what athletes do, but in the end, your goals aren't really so much different from theirs. You want to get as fit as you can in as little time as possible, right? By focusing your training program, you can do just that.

Measuring your fitness

Every good fitness program needs good measuring tools. You've got one of the essentials right here in the form of this training diary. The other two you can buy at almost any sporting goods store — a watch with a stopwatch function and a heart-rate monitor. They form what a consultant might call a synergy.

  ✔ The watch tells you how long you worked out.

  ✔ The heart-rate monitor tells you how hard you worked.

  ✔ The training diary lets you keep track of your progress.

And all three together will motivate you to get out, identify your strengths and weaknesses, and help you get the most out of your training time.

While timing your workout is pretty basic, heart-rate monitoring was something that, until recently, only elite athletes did. At its most fundamental level, your heart rate is really the measuring stick of your cardiovascular fitness. If your speed goes up while your heart rate stays the same, then, congratulations, you're fitter. But even more importantly, your heart rate is the most reliable indicator of how your body is producing energy, which gives you the opportunity to target your training that much more accurately.

And while you can take your pulse by just putting a finger on an artery on your wrist or on your neck, while you're exercising, it's far more convenient to just peek at your heart-rate monitor.

"But," you say, "I'm not an Olympic athlete." All the more reason why you need a heart-rate monitor. Olympic athletes actually have sort of a built-in heart-rate monitor, a sixth sense about how hard they're working, developed over years of training. They mostly use their heart-rate monitors to confirm what their bodies are already telling them.

Ironically, recreational athletes, who can benefit most from a heart-rate monitor, are the least likely to own one. Newbies are more likely to judge their workout by speed rather than real workload, so they're likely to overdo it if they encounter a hill and loaf a little when they've got a tail wind.

Do you fall into that camp? Try this test: During your next workout, guess your heart rate. If you're not consistently within 10 beats, you need a heart-rate monitor.

 Having trouble getting a reading from your heart-rate monitor early in your workout? Try licking the sensor. Most rely on the conductivity of your sweat to work properly, and saliva is the best substitute.

Maxing out — speaking from the heart

One bit of information that you need before you start on a training program is your *maximum heart rate*. Throughout the rest of this chapter, different training intensities are expressed as a percentage of maximum heart rate. Here's the simplest way to determine your MHR:

- ✔ Women, subtract your age from 226. (A 33-year-old female would end up with a maximum heart rate of 193.)

- ✔ Men, subtract your age from 220. (A 33-year-old male calculates a maximum heart rate of 187.)

 While this number should give you a reasonable ballpark rate, it doesn't take into account factors such as heredity and your present fitness level.

The other way of determining your maximum heart rate is by pushing yourself until you get there. The safest and most accurate way to do this is with a treadmill stress test administered by your doctor. And of course, before embarking on any exercise program, you should consult your doctor.

The Building Blocks of Training

So what's the difference between a planned workout and just plain exercising? Well, in a planned workout, you build at least one of three things: strength, speed, or endurance.

These are the building blocks of all fitness — whether it's on a bike, a basketball court, or a skating rink. Every sport more strenuous than chess calls upon these three basic qualities in various proportions. But before I talk about how to build your fitness, I need to define the terms.

Endurance

Endurance is a pretty straightforward concept. It's the ability to run or ride or swim a little further today than you did yesterday. Sure, some part of endurance is mental — it's a borderline obsessiveness that allows people to swim the English Channel or run an ultramarathon. But it's also physical attribute, the ability of your muscles and your connective tissues to keep going . . . and going . . . and going.

And for endurance efforts, your body produces energy *aerobically* — taking in as much oxygen as it's consuming — and uses fat as its primary fuel.

Strength

Simply, strength is the ability to move mass, but it's more than just the ability to move a refrigerator or do 100 pushups. In most forms of exercise, whether it's swimming, running, or cycling, the mass that you're moving is, well, you. And improving your strength gives you the ability to move further with every stride or stroke, as well as the ability to contend with natural obstacles such as head winds and hills.

For these kind of high-power activities, your body often functions *anaerobically* — you're consuming more oxygen than you can take in — and uses carbohydrates for quick energy.

A buyer's guide to heart-rate monitors

A heart-rate monitor should have a readout that's big enough to read while you're exercising. The buttons should be big enough that you can manipulate them while you're on the go. The elastic chest strap, which actually takes the reading, should be comfortable both while you're at rest and while you're exercising. The most important function is the capability to set a target heart-rate range with an audible alarm that beeps when you're above or below it.

As for the more sophisticated programming options — anything from a post-workout readout of average heart rate to a full record of the workout that can be downloaded to your computer — let your love of gadgetry, or lack thereof, be your guide.

Speed

Speed is, you guessed it, the ability to move fast. And it's easy to measure, whether against a rival or against the clock. Simply, if you have any thoughts about competing, whether seriously or casually, you have the need for speed.

Speed workouts are usually highly anaerobic and use carbohydrate stores as a fuel source.

The Three Kinds of Workouts

Okay, so you understand what your goals are. Now how do you tailor an aerobic program to increase your abilities? Well for starters, your master plan should incorporate three different kinds of workouts, each addressing one of the three cornerstones discussed in the preceding section.

Long, steady distance

To improve your endurance, you're going to do *LSD* — long, steady distance. By building endurance, LSD workouts provide a base for your training schedule. They train your body to use fat as a fuel, which is the most efficient way to power your muscles for long-distance workouts. They also allow your body to recover from the stresses that your power- and speed-building workouts place on your body.

LSD workouts seem easy, and in a way, that's the problem. You feel like you should be doing more, and so you push yourself beyond the point at which you're getting maximum training benefit. Discipline yourself to go slowly and keep your heart rate in the target range. Shoot for between 50 and 70 percent of your maximum heart rate on LSD workouts.

Strength training

While you can increase your strength by doing resistance workouts — running in sand, riding up hills, skating with really rusty bearings — the best way to get stronger is to hit the gym. A balanced whole-body program of weight lifting can increase your strength, help prevent injury, and even help you look better in a bathing suit.

It doesn't really matter whether you choose a machine-to-machine circuit or a series of light free-weight exercises. If you've never lifted weights before, ask a trainer at your gym or health club to show you proper form and help you design a workout plan. The key is stick-to-itiveness. It'll take about 12 to 16 weeks, working out two to three times a week, to really build your strength.

Unless your goal is to get pumped up Schwarzenegger-style, you should stay away from heavy weight/low rep exercises. Adding too much upper-body muscle could actually slow you down by adding a little power and a lot of extra weight.

Speed intervals

To get fast, you need to do sprint intervals. The idea is to run or pedal or swim as fast as you can for a short time — between 10 and 20 seconds. Then catch your breath and do it all over again.

In every muscle, there are fast-twitch and slow-twitch fibers. While an individual's proportion of fast-twitch to slow-twitch fibers is largely determined by genetics — Olympic sprinters got there by choosing their parents well — you can increase

Failing to succeed

How hard should you be pushing yourself during a sprint? Harder. No, harder than that. No, even harder. Elite athletes do intervals until "failure." What does that mean exactly? It means that on your last set, you can barely stand up, or take one more stroke.

On a micro level, you have tried and you have failed. And on a macro level, you have most definitely succeeded.

your percentage of fast-twitch fibers somewhat with speed training. Your heart rate should go completely into the anaerobic zone, the place where your body pulls out all its energy trump cards. This corresponds to a reading of between 85 and 100 percent of maximum heart rate.

Building a Workout Plan

In order to maintain a consistent workout regimen, you need to get out your calendar. What follows is a 12-week training program, divided into three phases, that's guaranteed to get you in top shape in as little time as possible.

✔ Phase 1 of the program focuses on building an endurance base (see Table 1-2). You start out working out three days a week, all LSD workouts. By the end of this phase, you're exercising four days a week and are doing some strength workouts.

✔ Phase 2 of the program focuses on maintaining your endurance while building your power (see Table 1-3). You start out with one weight workout a week and increase it to two, while introducing some speed work by the end of phase two.

✔ Phase 3 of the program focuses on maintaining your strength and endurance, while adding some speed work (see Table 1-4).

Table 1-2 — Workout Plan: Phase 1

Week	Sun	Mon	Tue	Wed	Thu	Fri	Sat
1	45 min LSD	Rest	Rest	30 min LSD	Rest	Rest	20 min LSD
2	60 min LSD	Rest	Rest	30 min LSD	Rest	Rest	25 min LSD
3	60 min LSD	Rest	20 min LSD	Rest	30 min LSD	Rest	30 min LSD
4	75 min LSD	Rest	30 min Strength	Rest	30 min LSD	Rest	30 min LSD

Table 1-3 — Workout Plan: Phase 2

Week	Sun	Mon	Tue	Wed	Thu	Fri	Sat
5	75 min LSD	Rest	Rest	Strength	Rest	40 min LSD	Rest
6	90 min LSD	Rest	Rest	Strength	Rest	40 min LSD	Rest
7	100 min LSD	Rest	Strength	Rest	40 min LSD	Rest	30 min Strength
8	100 min LSD	Rest	30 min Speed	Rest	50 min LSD	Rest	Strength

Table 1-4 — Workout Plan: Phase 3

Week	Sun	Mon	Tue	Wed	Thu	Fri	Sat
9	30 min Strength	Rest	30 min Speed	Rest	40 min LSD	Rest	110 min LSD
10	40 min Strength	Rest	30 min Speed	Rest	40 min LSD	Rest	110 min LSD
11	40 min Strength	Rest	40 min Speed	Rest	50 min LSD	Rest	110 min LSD
12	50 min Strength	Rest	40 min Speed	Rest	50 min LSD	Rest	110 min LSD

What do you do when you've reached week 12? Try the maintenance week schedule in Table 1-5 for a few weeks, which replaces one of the speed workouts with an LSD workout.

Table 1-5		Workout Plan: Maintenance				
Sun	*Mon*	*Tue*	*Wed*	*Thu*	*Fri*	*Sat*
90 min LSD	Rest	40 min Speed	Rest	50 min LSD	Rest	40 min Strength

No, the program isn't carved in stone, and you can feel free to adapt this training plan to your schedule and your level of fitness. However, note that there are some overriding principles in any good training program:

✔ You should alternate weight lifting or speed workouts with LSD days or rest days to allow for recovery.

✔ Longer LSD workouts fall on a Saturday or a Sunday, which gives you more flexibility in scheduling them.

✔ Your aerobic output will increase from week to week, by no more than 25 percent a week during the endurance phase and no more than 15 percent a week during the power and speed phases.

Chapter 2

Just Warming Up

*A*lways be prepared. It's a good motto, even if you're not a Boy Scout. And prepared is exactly what you'll be, after reading this chapter. In these pages, you find out how to ensure that your workout will be, as the pharmaceutical companies say, safe, effective, and without unpleasant side effects.

In exercising, as in orienteering, a few minutes ahead of time spent in getting yourself and your body prepared can pay big dividends down the road, making your workouts both more efficient and fun, as well as preventing injuries.

But unlike, say, getting your knot-tying merit badge, preparing properly for your workout is easy, if not always obvious. In this chapter, I discuss how to dress for comfort and efficiency, how to warm up and stretch effectively, and how to make the most of your workout time. So are you ready to get ready?

Bringing the Right Equipment

One of the nice things about exercising is that for the most part, it's gear free. But just because you can go out and exercise with just what you can carry in a gym bag, doesn't mean that the right equipment won't make your life a little easier. Here's how.

The right shoe on the right foot

A brief story about athletic shoes. A few years back, I went to my orthopedic surgeon with plantar fasciitis — an inflammation of a tendon that made it feel like someone was plunging an ice pick into the bottom of my feet. First off, he did what any doctor would do: He prescribed some anti-inflammatories to alleviate the pain and some stretching exercises to keep the tendon flexible. Then he asked me a question: "What kind of shoes are you wearing?"

"Whatever's on sale," I responded.

He said, "With feet like yours, you should be wearing Brand X or Brand Y. Brand Z is pretty wide, like your foot, but they're not going to give you the support that you need."

I did the math. I had saved $10 on the last pair of running shoes I bought. And I was paying the doctor $200 for 15 minutes of his time.

So I went out and bought a pair of Brand X shoes. Fit great. More importantly, within a week, the plantar fasciitis was gone. And five years later, it's still gone. What more can you ask for?

While I can't guarantee that picking the right footwear will keep the doctor away, I think there's a lesson here. Take some time to research the right footwear for your feet. Read magazine reviews. Check out the manufacturers' Web sites. Ask the advice of other athletes, and, yes, even your orthopedic surgeon. And once you find a brand and a model that works, stick with it. A shoe can't be a bargain if it comes complete with a trip to the doctor.

Getting a brand new bag

Do you have a gym bag? Great. Oh, you mean you don't? Then put down the book and go buy one, right now. Or soon anyway.

The right gym bag — and by that I mean one that's right for you — can make your life much easier. How? A sensible bag keeps your gear organized, which allows you to squeeze in a workout in a time slot where you once did nothing but scramble around looking for your tights and your lock.

What makes a good bag? One that's the right size — big enough to carry everything you need comfortably, but not so big that you're tempted to throw in the proverbial kitchen sink. Try to pick a style that you won't be ashamed to, say, carry to work.

The biggest practical need in a good bag is a way to segregate your wet clothes from your dry ones. The best bags have a partition, or a zippered compartment to keep the wet just-worked-out-in sweats away from the dry wearing-to-the-big-meeting clothes. Another big bonus is a breathable fabric — anything from Gore-Tex to mesh — which allows your workout gear to dry without getting moldy. And smell-wise, a bag that breathes will make you and your friends breathe easier, too.

A Word about Workout Wear

Clothes may or may not make the man, but they *can* make your workout much more comfortable. And today's new generation of athletic wear is better than ever.

Indoor clothes

The all-cotton T-shirt has long been a staple of the athletic wardrobe. And there are good reasons for it. It's cheap. It's comfortable. And it's easy to launder. But the problem is that it also absorbs sweat like the proverbial mop, which can make it less than comfortable after half an hour of hard exercise.

For those reasons, you may want to consign those Gap T-shirts to your casual wardrobe and get something a little more sports-specific for your workouts.

New polyester and polyester-blend fibers don't absorb sweat as readily as cottons and they wick moisture from the skin to the exterior to where it can evaporate. Pretty cool, eh? That's exactly what you'll be if you give these new school threads a try. Pretty dry, too. Athletic clothes that do the wicking routine usually have a hang tag explaining how the gee-whiz fabric works.

Outdoor clothes

If you're working out outside, you've got another set of obstacles to contend with — Mother Nature. And the problem, of course, is that the same clothing that keeps you warm can make you sweat enough that you get chilled anyway. But thanks in large part to man-made fibers, that has all changed. Here's what to look for:

- **High peformance polyester base layers** can wick moisture away from your skin so that the moisture evaporates before it makes you cold.

- **Fleece insulation layers** can keep you warm without bulk, and because they don't absorb moisture, they also won't get sweat-logged.

- **Breathable outer layers,** like shell jackets or pullovers, can protect you from the wind and rain (but not the gloom of night). The real trick is that these advanced fabrics, coupled with venting systems such as underarm zippers, allow enough air circulation so that you not only stay dry from the inside but also from the outside.

Why tights?

Sure, there's something sexy about skintight fabric over a trim body, but don't assume that its form-fitting cut is just for show. Recent studies have shown that tights made of Lycra or some other highly stretchy material can actually help to prevent muscle pain.

Essentially, the fabric exerts a mild compression on your leg muscles, which reduces the vibration that can cause muscle fatigue, as well as minimizes any inflammation if you overdo it. In short, your tights are working the same way as a pair of support hose does, or those burst-of-energy panty hose.

But don't overdo it. If your tights are too tight, it can constrict your circulation, and you could even injure yourself trying to wriggle inside. How tight is too tight? If it takes you longer to squirm into and out of your workout clothes than it does to actually work out, that's a hint that you need the next-larger size.

Warming Up to Warming Up

Do you have insurance on your house? On your car? Well, think of a good warm-up as insurance for your workout. Taking a few minutes before your workout to warm up can help prevent injuries and, yes, even boost your performance.

The pre-stretch warm-up

When I hurt my knee a few years back, I went to physical therapy to rehab it, and each session was like a gym workout on steroids — figuratively, of course. And the first thing my physical therapist did every session was put me on the stationary bike for about 15 minutes. Then, and only then, did we start a thorough and lengthy stretching routine before we hit the weights.

Why?, I asked. First, my therapist replied, contrary to popular opinion, stretching doesn't really warm up your muscles. What it takes to increase the circulation to the muscles and the connective tissue is some light aerobic exercise.

Secondly, serious stretching is important, but it isn't risk free. Overly enthusiastic stretching of cold muscles and joints is almost as likely to *cause* an injury as it is to prevent one.

And after filing this advice away, I began to notice this pre-stretching warm-up as one of the biggest differences between professional athletes and the rest of us. Watch recreational athletes, and the first thing they'll do is get down and start to stretch. But watch pros prepare for a game, and you'll find that the team trainers make them begin their workouts with a brief round of aerobic exercise, and only after they've begun to work up a sweat do they begin to stretch.

Here are some activities you can try to get the blood circulating, literally:

- ✔ **Pedal a stationary bike:** It's an easy, low-impact workout that works your whole leg. Just remember to keep the RPMs high and the resistance very low.

- ✔ **Take a light jog:** Again, it's important to hold yourself back. You're not doing aerobic work, you're just trying to increase your heart rate.

✔ **Take a walk:** No, it's not sexy, but a brisk walk is a good way to get the old blood circulating. And if you're really resourceful, you can combine it with transportation, walking to the gym or the beginning of your workout route.

If those ideas don't float your boat, just try something else to start the blood flowing. It doesn't really matter what you do as long as you keep the brakes on, so to speak, and don't go from breaking a sweat to working up a sweat.

Protecting your skin

When you're exercising outside, it's important to protect your skin. Some simple preventative measures can not only reduce the risk of premature aging but also serious, and increasingly common, problems such as skin cancer. The following are a few common-sense suggestions on ways to keep from tanning your hide:

✔ **Use sunscreen:** Your first line of defense is a sports-specific sunscreen that won't rub off when you sweat or sting if it drips into your eyes. And make sure the SPF is at least 30. Apply it on all exposed skin whenever you're exercising outside. And, yes, that means even on overcast days, when 70 percent of the sun's damaging rays still get through.

✔ **Cover up:** While it's smart to consider your clothes a critical line of defense against the sun, understand that a lot of workout wear isn't very high on the SPF scale. A white cotton T-shirt gernerally comes in at an SPF of 10 or less. So if you're exercising on a day when the sun is intense, or in a sun-intense environment such as when you're running on the beach, it's smart to apply sunscreen underneath your clothes.

The Power of Stretching

For most of us, stretching has always been one of those things that you do because it's good for you — the athletic equivalent of eating your vegetables. And it's true that stretching prevents injury. But believe it or not, stretching can actually improve your performance, too.

A warm knee is a happy knee

Admit it. You like showing off your legs. Most athletes do. And while it does good things for your ego, it may not be doing good things for your joints.

Your knee, you see, is lubricated by something called synovial fluid. "If the knee joint gets cold, it makes the synovial fluid thicker," says a sports scientist with USA Cycling.

"Normally, it's the consistency of warm honey. When it gets cold out, it's like cold honey, and it doesn't work so well." How cold is cold? Well, most European coaches make their riders wear tights or leg warmers anytime the temperature drops below 70°F. If you've got chronic knee problems, you may just want to do the same.

Here's how it works. According to Dr. Vijay Vad, an orthopedic surgeon at New York's Hospital for Special Surgery, as you get older the tendons that connect your muscles to your bones lose elasticity, kind of like a rubber band that's been left out in the sun too long. And as this happens, it restricts your ability to make the kind of explosive movements that you need to sprint or jump. (And, yes, this loss of the tensile properties in your tendons also makes you more susceptible to injury.)

The good news is that a program of slow, sustained stretching can actually restore much of the elasticity to your tendons, and in the process make you not only more limber, but more powerful, too. Here are a series of great upper- and lower-body stretches to get you started.

Lower body stretches

In most exercises, your legs are in constant motion. A stretching routine can not only increase your range of motion, and reduce the risk of muscle pulls, but can prevent or alleviate overuse injuries like tendinitis. Of course, you can feel free to supplement these stretches with your own favorites.

> ✔ **Quad stretch:** Standing upright, and holding onto something for balance if necessary, bring the heel of one foot up to your butt and grab your ankle with your hand. Gently pull the ankle up until you feel a stretch in your quadriceps (the muscles on the front of your thigh). Hold that position for 30 seconds and repeat with the other leg. (See Figure 2-1.)

> ✔ **Hamstring stretch:** While sitting on the ground, extend one leg in front of you and bend the other leg, keeping the inside of your knee on the floor. Lean forward and grab the ankle of the extended leg. Don't curl your neck down, but try to move your chin toward your toes. You should feel a stretch in your hamstrings (the muscles on the backs of your thighs). Hold that position, without bouncing, for 30 seconds, and then repeat on the other leg.

Figure 2-1: The quad stretch.

✔ **A-stretch:** Stand with your feet spread apart about as far as they'll go. Slowly bend one knee until you feel a stretch on the inside of your non-bent leg. Hold for 30 seconds. (See Figure 2-2.)

✔ **Calf stretch:** Step forward with your right foot as if doing a lunge. Bend your forward knee (keep your back leg straight) until you feel a stretch in the opposite calf. Hold that position for 30 seconds and then stretch the opposite leg. (Using a wall or some other object to lean against, you can stretch both calves at once, as in Figure 2-3.)

Figure 2-2: The A-stretch.

Figure 2-3: A double calf stretch.

✔ **Achilles stretch:** Stand with the balls of your feet on a step, but with your arches and heels dangling over. Hold onto a handrail for balance. Gently lower yourself until you feel a stretch in your Achilles tendons, just above the backs of your ankles. Hold that position for 30 seconds.

Upper body stretches

In most exercises, your upper body is especially subject to acute injury, from pulled muscles to more serious problems like ruptured discs and torn rotator cuffs. These stretches — along with any others you'd care to add — can help you reduce the risk of a trip to the doctor's office.

✔ **Hip stretch:** Lie flat on your back. Bend one leg up, grab your knee with both hands, and gently pull it toward your opposite shoulder. You should feel a stretch in your hips and buttocks. Hold the position for 30 seconds, again, not bouncing. Repeat on the other leg.

✔ **Lower back stretch:** Lie flat on the floor, face down, with your legs straight and your arms extended. Pull your hands underneath you so that you raise your shoulders off the floor, but keep your hips on the ground. You should feel a stretch in your lower back. Hold for 30 seconds.

✔ **Upper back stretch:** Lie face-down with your legs extended and your hands next to your shoulders as if you were going to do a push-up. Move your hips off the floor, while keeping your knees and shins on the ground. Then move your hips back until your arms are fully extended, and you feel a stretch in your upper back between your shoulder blades. Hold for 30 seconds.

✔ **Shoulder stretch:** While standing with back straight, reach across your torso with your right hand and grasp your left upper arm. Allow the left arm to bend. Slowly, pull the left arm until you feel a gentle stretch in that shoulder. Hold for 30 seconds, then reach with your left hand across your body and grab your right upper arm. Pull and stretch.

✔ **Forearm stretch:** Hold your right arm straight in front of you, extending from the shoulder and keeping your elbow straight. Raise your hand at the wrist, until your fingers are pointing straight up. The position is as though you were giving someone a stop sign. Hold for 15 seconds. Lower your hand until your fingers are pointing straight down. Hold for 15 seconds, then repeat the stretch with your left arm.

No pain/no gain does not apply to stretching. Stretching shouldn't hurt. If you reach the point of pain, you may be injuring yourself, so back off a little.

Too sick to exercise? Maybe not . . .

You've got a lousy head cold, and, well, you're just not feeling like yourself. Should you bag your workout? It depends. If you're running a fever, or if you've got a hacking cough or significant chest congestion, you should wait until you get better. But if you've got the common cold, or a touch of the flu, you don't necessarily have to stay in bed.

Research has shown that light to moderate exercise can actually boost your immune system and help you fight off whatever's bugging you. The key, of course, is to make the workout mellow — a light jog is fine, but running dozens of wind sprints will probably just make you sicker. Just as important, help your body regulate its temperature. If the thermometer is below freezing, consider running on the treadmill instead of around the park. And when you're done, get out of those wet clothes so that you don't get chilled, which, old wives' tales to the contrary, won't make you sick, but can make you more sick by reducing your body's ability to fight off germs and viruses.

Chapter 3

Running the Right Way

*P*ut one foot in front of the other. Repeat as necessary. That's one of running's great joys: its utter simplicity. Lacing up your shoes and hitting the road is a great excuse to forget about car payments and prospects for world peace. Just put your body in overdrive and your brain in neutral for a little while.

But while running is splendidly simple, it's not a no-brainer. You've got important decisions to make about where and when to run, what to wear, how far and how fast to go. And there are plenty of big and small ways that you can improve your performance, prevent injury, and simply have more fun on your run. After all, anything worth doing is worth doing right.

So with that in mind, this chapter is chock full of tips and techniques that you can take along with you on your next run. And check out *Running For Dummies* for even more tips.

Choosing Your Pace

So how fast should you run? "Fast enough, but not too fast," isn't going to cut it. The pace of your run should depend on what you're trying to accomplish. Here's a breakdown of a variety of run workouts and what you should be able to accomplish with them.

Going long with LSD

Dr. Timothy Leary notwithstanding, in the running world *LSD* stands for *long, steady distance.* LSD runs are done over a long distance at a slow aerobic pace to help you build endurance. LSD runs are really the bedrock of any training program, because they allow you to build mileage at a low intensity that will keep soreness and injury at bay.

The biggest challenge of LSD runs is actually keeping the pace down, because even brief high-intensity efforts sabotage the benefits of LSD training.

- ✔ **Sample workout:** Obviously, going long means something different to every runner, but 30 minutes is a good place to start. LSD workouts should be totally aerobic — your body shouldn't be consuming oxygen more quickly than you can take it in.

- ✔ **Heart rate:** Your target heart rate should be between 50 and 70 percent of your maximum heart rate. (See Chapter 1 for more about determining your maximum heart rate.) At first, you may have to alternate running and walking to keep your heart rate that low.

Having fun with fartlek

Swedish for speedplay, *fartlek* runs help build speed in race-like conditions. The idea is pretty simple. Start out at a moderate pace — a tempo run — but at random intervals, pick up the pace sharply for some predetermined distance, and then slow back down to tempo pace. The first segment may consist of a quick 50-yard sprint to the next telephone pole. The next segment may be 200 yards at a more moderate pace.

If it sounds a little unstructured, it is. That's because races tend to be unstructured, too. The idea is to get used to brief anaerobic efforts — you're using oxygen faster than you can replenish it — and being able to return to your race pace.

- ✔ **Sample workout:** Start with a run pace that's somewhere between an LSD run and a race pace run, and then add sprints that range from 20 yards to as much as 200 yards.

> ✔ **Heart rate:** During the sprints, your heart rate may climb to 85 percent of your maximum heart rate, but for the bulk of the run, it should stay at about 70 percent of maximum.

Training at race pace

These workouts are just what the name implies. Figure out your target time for an event, then work it back to a per-mile pace. For example, if you want to run a 10K in 50 minutes, that divides out to an eight-minute-mile pace. So early on in your training schedule, you can start with a half mile, or if you can manage it, a mile at that race pace. Gradually, increase your race pace mileage until you're approaching the actual race distance. Race pace workouts are really draining, so don't do them more than once a week.

> ✔ **Sample workout:** If you're aiming to do a 10K in under 50 minutes, start out with a mile and a half run in 12 minutes, and then work up to runs that are closer to your target distance.

> ✔ **Heart rate:** Your heart rate at race pace should be right at the threshold between an aerobic and anaerobic effort, so don't exceed 80 to 85 percent of your maximum heart rate.

Revving up with intervals

To build pure speed, you need to head to the track. An *interval* is a flat-out, as-hard-as-you-can-go, sprint effort, followed by a light jog that helps you get your heart rate down to a target range, and then another sprint, until, well, you're ready to collapse. The goal is not only to build speed and strength, but improve your running form. But when you can out-kick your neighbor in the last 100 yards of that 10K, all that hard work will be worth it.

> ✔ **Sample workout:** You may want to start with four 50-yard sprints, with, say, a minute of recovery time after each one. As you develop speed and strength, you can increase both the distance and the number of intervals.

✔ **Heart rate:** While you're sprinting, your target heart rate should be between 85 and 100 percent of your maximum heart rate, but it should dip back down to 80 percent or lower during your recovery periods.

A Word about Running Shoes

Your body can take a real pounding when you run. With every step, your feet hit the ground with an impact that measures in the thousands of pounds. And your running shoes are the only thing that comes between you and the road. So it's important to have good shoes.

Essentially, a running shoe does two things. First, the foam midsole provides cushioning against all that impact. Some shoes even incorporate gel- or air-filled pockets. However, be careful about buying the cushiest shoes you can find, because they can add unnecessary weight and actually compromise support.

A good shoe also provides support and motion control. The biggest problem for most runners is *over-pronating* — an excessive rolling inward during your stride. A few runners, particularly those with high arches, have the opposite problem — rolling outward, or *supinating*. When you're shoe shopping, be sure to bring your old shoes so that the salesperson can examine the wear patterns for evidence of either problem.

The problem, of course, is that no shoe is all things to all runners. While asking other runners and reading reviews in running magazines is a good place to start, finding the right shoes is largely a matter of trial and error. Once you find a pair of shoes that works for you, stick with them.

Remember, shoes don't last forever, and the foam cushioning layers in the midsole, as well as the support systems of the uppers, will often wear out before the outsole. If you've been using your shoes regularly for more than six months, it's probably time for a new pair.

Building an Efficient Stride

The Road Runner was right. The most efficient way to run is to take lots of fast little strides, and not just lope along Wile E. Coyote-style. Sports scientists suggest that by keeping your feet close to the ground and moving forward instead of up, you can shave precious seconds off your race times. To tack another half mile onto your morning runs, you can shorten your strides — even by a few inches — and up your *RPMs* (revolutions per minute).

Most recreational runners average about 80 strides per minute, while top middle distance runners have stride rates of over 100.

One of the best places to practice this striding adjustment is on a treadmill, where you can look at your watch and count your strides without having to worry about cars, curious dogs, or uneven pavement.

Choosing Your Running Surface

What's under your feet really does make a difference. Finding the right running surface can help prevent injuries and make running a lot more fun. Here's a look at the pros and cons of some popular surfaces.

Concrete

This surface is as hard as a rock, because that's literally what it's made of. That means that those light grey roads and the sidewalks in your neighborhood aren't the best places for a run. Concrete has almost no give underfoot, so it's not only hard on your feet, but your knees, hips, and back as well.

Asphalt

Although most of us think that a road is a road, both paving crews and your feet know better. Asphalt is much softer than concrete — especially in warmer weather — and makes for a much friendlier running surface. So if you've got a choice between concrete and asphalt, head for the blacktop.

Dirt trails

Dirt trails in a park not only make for a scenic diversion but also a relatively cushy surface underfoot. The drawback is that trails are often uneven, pocked with small holes, tree roots, and small rocks. So to keep from turning an ankle, try to hit the trail in midday when the light is good and the obstacles are most visible.

Cinder tracks

Well, if it's good enough for Jesse Owens, it's good enough for you. Cinder tracks — nowadays a thin, loose coat of fine gravel — may not be modern, but they're easy on your body. They're also common — almost every large park has one. Keep in mind that the softness of the surface will slow your times down, but that will only make you feel faster on race day.

Rubberized track

Just a couple of strides and you'll realize that rubberized tracks are like Tigger: bouncy, trouncy, flouncy, pouncy, fun, fun, fun, fun, fun. The thickness of the individual surface varies from track to track, but the combination of smoothness, flatness, and springiness makes this a great place to rack up some mileage. All-weather tracks may be a little hard to find — your local college might be your best bet — but are well worth seeking out.

Running Safely

There's a reason why they call it road racing. Many runners put in their miles on the same thoroughfares where Fords and Volvos run free. The problem with that, of course, is that roads weren't designed with two-footed recreation in mind. Here are some tips for coexisting safely with motor vehicles:

✔ **Stick to the shoulder:** Running in the path of traffic is simply looking for trouble. Stay as far to the side of the road as possible, but be careful for debris that may be found on the shoulder.

✔ **Face oncoming traffic:** Always run facing traffic rather than with the flow of traffic so that you can see — and avoid — any vehicles that might not be able to see you.

✔ **Assume you're invisible:** Many drivers simply don't see anything — or anyone — that doesn't have a license plate and weighs less than 2,000 pounds. So don't assume that because a driver is looking in your general direction, he'll see and avoid you. Remember, if you're wrong, you'll have much bigger problems than higher insurance rates.

✔ **Wear bright colors:** Sure, black is basic, but bright-colored shirts, singlets, or jackets make it easier for you to be seen.

Running at Night

One of the great things about running is that it can be done in the dark. Being able to train late at night or first thing in the morning makes it much easier to squeeze a run into your busy schedule. But there are a few safety considerations for nocturnal workouts.

✔ **Buddy up:** For the same reason you feel safer walking a dark street when you're not alone, you should feel the same way about running. Recruiting a friend will not only make you feel better but also probably reduce your chances of running into trouble.

✔ **Find a smooth and well-lighted place:** Because you can't look where you're going if you can't see where you're going, make sure that the place you pick for your night-time run is well lighted. And after dark is no time to take up trail running — look for a smooth surface that's far less likely to cause injury.

✔ **And one's that lightly trafficked:** Cars are even more of a problem at night. You should wear a reflective vest, and maybe even a small battery powered light to help make sure that cars see you.

Hitting the weights

Want to improve your times without increasing your mileage one iota? Head to the gym. A balanced program of weight lifting can increase your strength and speed, help prevent injury, and even help you look better in a bathing suit. Your goal should be a basic whole-body workout in the form of a machine-to-machine circuit or a series of light freeweight exercises.

If you've never lifted weights before, ask a trainer at your gym or club to show you proper form and help you design a workout plan. The key is stick-to-itiveness. It'll take about 12 to 16 weeks, working out two to three times a week, to really build your strength. You can also check out *Weight Training For Dummies* for tips and techniques to get you started, as well as *The Weight Training Diary For Dummies* if you really get into weight lifting.

As a runner, your goal isn't to get pumped up Schwarzenegger-style, so stay away from heavy weights and low reps. Adding too much upper body muscle could actually slow you down by adding a little power and a lot of extra weight.

Racing in the Streets

One of the coolest things about running is that you can compete in races virtually from day one, without devoting your whole life to training. Here's what you need to know to get started competing.

Why should I race?

Good question. Actually, every racer has his or her own reasons for sending in that entry fee and setting the alarm on Sunday morning. Here are some of the most universal:

- ✔ **Fun:** Races, especially small ones, are a real social event, with a lot of the same people running the same events year after year.

- ✔ **Motivation:** Having a few races scheduled throughout the year gives you a reason to get out of bed at 6 a.m. and lace up your running shoes.

✔ **Accomplishment:** Even if you're not near the front of the pack, you can feel like a winner when you lower your personal best time.

✔ **Speed:** Take this to the bank: When you pin that number on and stand at the line waiting for the crack of the starter's pistol, you're only minutes away from your best time. The adrenaline factor — not to mention the I-want-to-beat-the-guy-in-the-orange-singlet factor — will help you find physical and mental reserves that you didn't know you had, and make the miles glide by faster than they ever do in training.

What distance should I choose?

When picking a race, there is a wide variety of distances to choose from. Here's a quick rundown of some popular races from short to long.

✔ **Road mile:** This classic track distance has now hit the road and is becoming increasingly popular for runners looking for a fast-paced change from 5K and 10K races.

✔ **5K:** While it's often the first distance that beginning runners tackle, the 5K can also be a demanding race for accomplished runners. Endurance isn't enough to clock a really good 5K time; speed is also a necessary ingredient.

✔ **10K:** This 6.2-mile road race is the most popular distance among recreational racers, with good reason. It's long enough to present a challenge and to minimize the necessity for speed training. But it's also short enough that you don't need a year's worth of training to compete.

✔ **Half marathon:** As you might expect, this 13.1-mile race is most popular among racers working their way up to a full marathon distance.

✔ **Marathon:** Yes, we all know about the poor Greek messenger who ran the first marathon and promptly dropped dead. But that was then and this is now, with runners of all ability levels tackling this 26.2-mile endurance test.

Should I have a race strategy?

It's not exactly mapping out a zone defense in football, but running a good race does entail some strategy and preparation, both mental and physical. Here are some hints to help you run your best time:

- ✔ **Have a plan:** As Elaine said to Benjamin in *The Graduate,* "I don't want you to go . . . until you have a plan." Before you head to the starting line you should have a target time. But make sure that it's realistic. Trying to run 30 seconds faster than your best 5K? That's realistic. Trying to break 20 minutes when you've never broken 25? Fuggedaboudit.

- ✔ **Start slowly:** It's really easy to get caught up in the excitement of the moment and go out too fast. Going anaerobic in the first half mile is a recipe for disaster. So consciously slow your pace over the first mile, and check your time at the first distance marker so that you can make sure you're running as slowly as you think you are.

- ✔ **Don't forget to hydrate**: In a longer race, anything over 5K, make sure that you plan for water stops. It's especially important to drink early, chugging some water before you're thirsty. In longer races — half marathon distance and up — make sure to consume a few calories as well.

- ✔ **Sticking to your pace:** First off, before you start you should know what mile splits you have to hit in order to achieve your target time. Believe me, it's tough doing division in your head while you're running. And once you settle into your race groove, try not to get distracted by subjective factors, such as how you feel or the pace of your fellow runners. Your stopwatch and your heart-rate monitor are much more objective judges of whether you should speed up or slow down.

- ✔ **Finish strong:** Sure you're tired. But you'll have plenty of time to rest after you cross the finish line. So over the race's last mile, pick up the pace. And when the finish line is in sight, that's the time for a full-on sprint. You might catch a couple of fading front-runners, shave a few seconds off your time, and give you the satisfaction that you gave all you had to give.

The Mental Side of Racing

If you're running as hard as you should be, you'll probably have some moments during the race when you're feeling pretty bad. This is when your mental resolve comes into play. Follow these guidelines and you'll be able to sail through those bad patches and finish with a personal best.

- **Think positively:** Is the race half over, or do you still have half the race to run? The most successful runners are optimists, able to put a positive spin even on a tough situation.

- **Remember the Alamo:** As Nietzsche said, "That which does not kill you makes you strong." So when you're facing a crisis, marshal your resources by remembering your toughest races and how you plowed through those few rough patches to finish strong.

- **Be your own drill sergeant:** Sometimes a tough-love approach is what you need. Remind yourself about how hard you trained, and if you even think about dropping out, soldier, you're going to put yourself on KP duty so fast your head'll spin. Got it?

- **Distract yourself:** It's really easy to get wrapped up in how bad you feel. So just try and dissociate yourself from your suffering. Hum a song. Try and remember lines from *The Godfather, Part II.* Look around for attractive runners of the gender of your choice. Think about anything but your labored breathing.

- **Make micro goals:** Don't think about the fact that you're four miles from the finish. Instead, say to yourself, I'm going to run hard until I get to the firehouse a quarter mile down the road. And after you reach the firehouse, find a new, easily achievable target.

Chapter 4

Cooling Down and Fueling Up

To paraphrase the novelist Dorothy Parker, I hate exercising, but I love having exercised. Okay, that's not quite true. While the act of exercising often involves significant discomfort, there are few things in this world that compare with the afterglow of having just completed a great workout.

But while it's tempting to kick back as soon as you're done sweating, resist the temptation. The truth is, the minute your last workout is over, the preparation for your next workout is beginning.

The good news is that a lot of that preparation is fun — it involves high-on-the-hit-parade activities like eating, drinking, resting, and gloating over your accomplishments.

In this chapter, I discuss how to cool down, eat right, replenish your fluids, and rest the right way.

The Cool-Down

Did you ever watch the Kentucky Derby? Do the horses slam on the brakes as soon as they cross the finish line? Of course not. Well, you shouldn't either. After your workout, you need a few minutes to allow your body to make a smooth and gradual transition from exercise to rest.

You need to give your heart rate an opportunity to slow from its exercise-induced frenzy to a calmer, resting rate. A cool-down also gives your muscles the opportunity to flush out the lactic acid — the by-product of anaerobic exercise that's commonly known as liquid pain — that would otherwise make you oh-so-sore the next morning.

So how do you achieve this graceful progression from the sweating state to the post-sweating state? Simple. Just slow down. If you're doing an aerobic exercise, simply taper down your speed and resistance. If you're running, slow to a jog, and then to a walk. If you're swimming, slow down your stroke. If you're on a bicycle, shift down a gear or two and gradually pedal more slowly. Most exercise machines that you'll find in the gym — stair climbers, elliptical trainers, and stationary bikes — do this for you by building in a cool-down period at the end of each pre-programmed workout.

As a rule of thumb, five minutes is a good length of time for a cool-down, which is why most machines have this length of time pre-programmed. But listen to your body, too, and feel free to extend your cool-down time after a particularly intense workout session.

The morning after

Do you ever feel at the peak of your soreness two days after a workout? There's a good reason for this. While the muscle pain you feel the day after exercise is largely caused by the aforementioned lactic acid buildup, the soreness you feel a couple of days later is caused by microtears in your muscles being repaired.

In moderate amounts, this pain is your body telling you that it's getting stronger. If you're experiencing so much pain that it's affecting your next workout, then it should be a signal for you to cut back. That old saying, "no pain, no gain," is right, but only to a point.

If you're doing resistance training, just shift to aerobic mode for a few minutes and jog, walk, or pedal for a few minutes to get your body in motion. A round of light post-workout stretching can also help your form.

Resting to Get Stronger

Here's the news you've been waiting for. If you want to get fitter, it's just as important to rest well as it is to work out hard. Elite athletes know this. They understand that while they're resting, their bodies are recovering from the day's exertion. "Recovery is just as important as the workout," says Steve Johnson, an exercise physiologist with USA Cycling. "The purpose of the workout is to stress the body and let it repair itself. The benefit of the workout only happens after you've recovered."

That's why it can be smart to make a workout plan that allows for a couple of nonconsecutive days off during the week, especially after a particularly hard workout, and restrict yourself to "active rest."

What's active rest? It's not vegging out on the couch or surfing the Web. It's moderate activity of the kind that you'd do to warm up for or cool down from a workout:

- Do some gentle stretching.
- Take a walk.
- Shoot a few baskets.
- Mow the lawn.

Active rest is anything that gets you moving without really breaking a sweat. This will keep your muscles from getting stiff and help get the blood circulating to the connective tissue in your hips, your knees, and your ankles. And as long as you take it easy, your body will be able to divert its energy reserves into helping repair the damage that yesterday's intense workout inflicted, and it will build stronger muscles in the process.

Refueling Your Body

You know the old saying, "You are what you eat." So do you really want to be a Big Mac, a large order of fries, and a chocolate shake the next time you hit the gym? When you're exercising, food isn't food, it's fuel. Which is why you need to think before you chew.

Eating before your workout

This is a balancing act. You need to eat enough to give you enough energy for your workout, but not so much that you end up slowing yourself down. In practical terms, proper pre-exercise fueling is mostly a matter of monitoring not only *how much* you eat, but also *what* you eat.

As you found out after you left the all-you-can-eat buffet at Enchilada World, some foods are more easily digested than others. Generally, this means focusing on easily-digested carbohydrates and keeping fats to a minimum. If you're working out in the morning, cereal or yogurt is a better bet than a triple cheese omelet with a side of sausage. (I found this one out the hard way on a particularly strenuous bicycle ride following a particularly indulgent brunch.) For lunch, smart fueling means bypassing the bacon double cheese-burger with a crème brûlée chaser and going for the pasta salad with the dressing on the side.

Why are foods that are okay when you're chilling out such a no-no when you're exercising? Chalk it up to evolution. Back in the days when your ancestors were being chased by saber-toothed tigers, they needed all the help they could get. So your body developed a response to this fight-or-flight situation. When you're running away from a woolly mammoth — or just pedaling up a big hill — your body funnels most of its resources to your muscles, postponing non-essential functions, like digestion. So eating easily digestible foods allows you to keep your muscles well-fueled and keeps your stomach from rebelling. In short, you could say that it's about staying on the right side of the line between eating and being eaten.

Eating during your workout

Should you eat during your workout? Probably not. If you're just going to the gym or for a short run, you can wait until you get home. But if you're running a half-marathon, or going on a 50-mile bike ride, you should plan for some on-the-go refueling. The key is to do it early, before your energy reserves run low, and in small amounts and in regular intervals so that it's easily digested.

No, I don't mean you should stop at the drive-through window. A couple of bites of an energy bar or a little bit of fruit is enough. And keep in mind, I'm defining eating in the broadest possible way — that is, taking in calories. So if you chug some fruit juice or a sports drink, as far as your body's concerned, that's eating.

 What should you eat? From a nutritional standpoint, it should be mostly carbohydrates, with a little bit of fat to mellow out the blood-sugar spike that can come from too much sugar. There is a multi-million-dollar industry trying to get you to choose energy bars and energy gels for your in-ride nutritional needs. They're generally easy to eat, and nutritionally, they've done most of the thinking for you. If you like the way they taste and they make you feel more like a triathlete, go right ahead. But they're not magic. You probably have some perfectly good energy foods in your kitchen cupboard, such as those in Table 4-1.

Table 4-1		Food for Exercise		
Food	*Calories*	*Carbohydrates*	*Fat*	*Protein*
4 fig bars	200	46 g	0 g	2 g
3 Rice Krispie treats	225	45 g	4.5g	1.5 g
1 Milky Way Lite bar	170	34 g	5 g	1 g
1 Power Bar	225	42 g	2.5 g	10 g
2 Bananas	220	58 g	0 g	2 g

The bonk

Are you one of those people who hates to stop at a gas station? You'll run your car until it's almost at E, right at E, and even a little bit below E. Did you ever push it too far? Well, when your body runs out of fuel during the middle of a long workout — more than an hour — it's called *the bonk*. While it sounds kind of fun, the symptoms aren't: sudden, extreme weakness, often accompanied by lightheadedness, nausea, and/or severe hunger.

Fortunately, it only happens during endurance events — triathlons, 100-mile bike rides, and marathon runs — and the prevention is simple: Eat before you exercise. Eat small amounts frequently while you're on the road. And don't wait until you feel hungry. By then, it's probably too late.

A linguistic note: In French, the bonk is called *la fringale,* a word so euphonic that a fine French restaurant in San Francisco adopted it as its name. Funny how the French can make something so unpleasant sound romantic.

As you can see, there's not all that much difference between performance food and what your mother would dismiss as junk food. All have a good amount of carbohydrates and an acceptably low level of fat, and they can be eaten easily while you're running or riding. And if you stop to eat, your choices widen even further.

Eating after your workout

As soon as you're done with your workout, head for the cupboard, and get some carbohydrates into your system. Energy bars or drinks, fruit, pretzels, just about anything will do. It's not the time for a full meal, but an important chance to replenish your energy reserves.

And the timing is important. For the first half-hour after your workout, your body is primed to replace the carbohydrates you used to power your muscles during your workout. Once that window of opportunity has passed, you simply can't top off your tank as effectively.

After a couple of hours, it's time for a full meal. Here's the time for that well-balanced diet with an eye toward your long-term energy needs. It's a good time to fuel up with protein — something lean, like a chicken breast, pork tenderloin, or piece of fish. Some veggies add fiber and all sorts of nutrients to the mix. Round out the meal with a small side of complex carbohydrates — a baked potato, a portion of pasta, or even just some bread. As for the fats, just keep it in perspective. In moderation, fats are a necessary part of a balanced diet. What that means is that while an occasional pat of butter or sprinkle of grated cheese won't hurt you, you should pass on the ribeye steak.

The Hydration Quotient

Do you ever get home from a workout, and before you step into the shower, you step on the scale? "Three pounds lighter than this morning," you congratulate yourself. While it's certainly gratifying to watch those numbers go down, the reality is that you're probably a little less fat and a whole lot dehydrated.

There are a lot of reasons why water is the most important nutrient there is. Water — in the form of sweat — helps your body regulate its core temperature, and if you don't replenish your body's supply, it's like running your car with the radiator only half full. When you mix dehydration with exertion, the result can be heat exhaustion and, even rarely, heat stroke. In its more moderate forms, dehydration can cause muscle cramping and even make you more susceptible to muscle pulls.

So drink. Lots. In the hours before your workout, remember to drink a couple of nice large glasses of water. As long as you're sticking to water, it's almost impossible to drink to excess.

Drinking while you exercise is almost a Zen thing. You need to drink before you're thirsty. If you wait until you're thirsty, you're already dehydrated, and you're fighting a losing battle. Plan to drink at least four ounces every fifteen minutes — more often if it's really hot — and you'll be fine.

And don't stop rehydrating after your exercise. In the hours after a workout, you'll still need to drink to rehydrate your body. It's also important to throw some electrolytes into the mix. Energy drinks help your body replenish these vital chemicals, but sensible eating — pretzels for sodium, a banana for potassium — can also do the job.

How can you tell if you're dehydrated? Well, if I may be so crude, simply look at the color of your urine. If it's clear, or almost clear, you're well hydrated. If it's dark yellow, hit the water fountain, now.

Are You Overtraining?

There is such a thing as too much of a good thing. If you don't believe me, ask the third runner-up in a hot-dog eating contest. The same goes for fitness. There's a fine line between building up and tearing down, and it's easy to veer onto the wrong side of it. How do you know if you're training too hard? Listen to your body. Do you feel chronically tired? Like you're constantly on the verge of getting sick? Are you having trouble sleeping?

Those admittedly vague symptoms can all be symptoms of overtraining, especially if you've increased the duration or intensity of your workouts in the past week or two. The best objective way to monitor your training is to check your resting heart rate before you get out of bed in the morning. If your exercise program is working, your resting heart rate should stay basically the same or even gradually drift slightly downward as your fitness increases. If you find that your resting heart rate has increased, it's a sure sign that your body's under stress.

Fortunately, unlike the common cold, there's a cure for overtraining. Just simply take a day or two off, and when you go back to training, take it a little easier until your first-thing-in-the morning heart rate settles back down.

Dealing with Injuries

Injuries are a part of athletics. Despite all your careful preparation, eventually you'll suffer some kind of an injury. The key, of course, is to treat the injury aggressively so that you can return to action as soon as possible.

Acute injuries

Ouch! That's the sign of an acute injury. One minute you're exercising and the next minute you're writhing in pain.

If you're experiencing severe pain, numbness, or restricted movement in a joint after a fall, see your doctor immediately to rule out a broken bone or a serious dislocation of the joint.

For less-serious orthopedic injuries — such as mild sprains or bruises — follow the RICE regimen (**R**est, **I**ce, **C**ompression, **E**levation) outlined later in this chapter, and if the injury doesn't heal within a reasonable period of time, see your doctor anyway.

Overuse injuries

Overuse injuries, on the other hand, tend to sneak up on you. You're a little sore one day, a little better the next, a little more sore the day after that. And then one day you wake up and you can't walk down the stairs.

To prevent overuse injuries, be smart and listen to your body. If you're training for an event, increase your workload gradually. If you're experiencing pain during or after exercise, take a few days off, or do some cross-training which will help you stay in shape without aggravating your injury. And if the pain is severe, or persists more than a few days, see your doctor.

Treating injuries

The basic and muscle injuries is pretty treatment for most joint and muscle injuries is pretty similar, regardless of the cause. The standard RICE regimen is the place to start:

- ✔ **R is for rest.** Stay off it — that means no weight-bearing exercises. Some recent research suggests that gentle, range-of-motion exercise can speed healing — call this active rest.

✔ **I is for Ice.** As soon as possible, put an ice pack on the affected area to keep down swelling and inflammation during the first 48 hours after an acute injury. Icing after exercise can help reduce pain and inflammation of an overuse injury.

✔ **C is for compression.** Wrap the joint to keep down the swelling and inflammation. In the case of an acute injury, it means not taking off a shoe or a glove or a pair of tights until you can get home to ice it. If it's an overuse injury, wrapping the area can provide support as well as help to reduce pain and inflammation.

✔ **E is for elevation.** Raise the affected body part to keep the swelling down.

After checking with your doctor, you can augment the RICE regimen by taking a non-prescription-strength anti-inflammatory (such as ibuprofen). Anti-inflammatories can not only ease the pain of injuries and muscle and joint soreness but also, more importantly, they can actually help promote healing by reducing swelling.

Part II
The Runner's Training Diary

The 5th Wave
By Rich Tennant

"This readout shows your heart rate, blood pressure, bone density, skin hydration, plaque buildup, liver function, and expected lifetime."

In this part . . .

Got your pen? Great. Because this is the part of the book that you write. The training diary pages in this section are your tabula rasa, a blank slate just waiting for you to record your goals, your accomplishments, and whatever else you'd like to put down on paper.

Your Training Diary

*T*his is the part of the book that you write yourself, a customizable workout log where you can list your personal goals and record your progress. It's this section that makes this book truly *your* book.

At a minimum, you should record how long you worked out, how many reps at each weight you did in the weight room, or the duration and distance of your aerobic workout. You may also want to record how you felt when you got up and before, during, and after your workout.

Use this diary in a way that works best for you, but remember that I've assumed that you may not work out every day of every week — in fact, a good workout plan includes a healthy balance of exercise and rest.

- ✔ Track your progress over a ten-day stretch.
- ✔ Customize your journal each day for whatever workout you choose for that day.
- ✔ Write down your personal training goals in the, er, Training Goals section.
- ✔ Celebrate your training accomplishments in the Workout Wrap-Up section.
- ✔ Track your diet and nutrition goals in the Food for Thought section.
- ✔ And don't forget to note how you felt during your workout and what you should focus on for your next training session.

"This is my job this year. Just like a job, there are days you don't want to go to work, but you do."
— Jerry Dunn, in July 2000 after breaking his own record of 104 marathons in a year, on his way to a goal of finishing 200 marathons

Training Goals

Goals!

Date:

Training	Time/Distance	Sets	Reps

Food for Thought

Date:

Training	Time/Distance	Sets	Reps

Food for Thought

Date:

Training	Time/Distance	Sets	Reps

Food for Thought

Date:

Training	Time/Distance	Sets	Reps

Food for Thought

Date:

Training	Time/Distance	Sets	Reps

Food for Thought

Date:

Training   Time/Distance   Sets   Reps

_____

_____

_____

_____

_____

Food for Thought

_____

_____

_____

Date:

Training   Time/Distance   Sets   Reps

_____

_____

_____

_____

_____

Food for Thought

_____

_____

_____

Date:

Training   Time/Distance   Sets   Reps

_____

_____

_____

_____

_____

Food for Thought

_____

_____

_____

Date:

Training	Time/Distance	Sets	Reps

Food for Thought

....

Date:

Training	Time/Distance	Sets	Reps

Food for Thought

Workout Wrap-Up

Accomplishments!	Notes

"Our most sacred convictions, the unchanging elements of our supreme values, are judgments of our muscles."
— *Friedrich Nietzsche, philosopher and writer*

Training Goals

Goals!

_____

_____

_____

_____

_____

....

Date:

Training	Time/Distance	Sets	Reps

Food for Thought

_____

_____

_____

....

Date:

Training	Time/Distance	Sets	Reps

Food for Thought

_____

_____

_____

Date:

Training	Time/Distance	Sets	Reps

Food for Thought

Date:

Training	Time/Distance	Sets	Reps

Food for Thought

Date:

Training	Time/Distance	Sets	Reps

Food for Thought

Date:

Training	Time/Distance	Sets	Reps

Food for Thought

Date:

Training	Time/Distance	Sets	Reps

Food for Thought

Date:

Training	Time/Distance	Sets	Reps

Food for Thought

Date:

Training	Time/Distance	Sets	Reps

Food for Thought

Date:

Training	Time/Distance	Sets	Reps

Food for Thought

Workout Wrap-Up

Accomplishments!	Notes

"What lies behind us and what lies before us are small matters compared to what lies within us."
— Ralph Waldo Emerson, writer and philosopher

Training Goals

Goals!

_____

_____

_____

_____

_____

....

Date:

Training	Time/Distance	Sets	Reps
_____	_____		
_____	_____		
_____	_____		
_____	_____		
_____	_____		

Food for Thought

_____

_____

_____

....

Date:

Training	Time/Distance	Sets	Reps
_____	_____		
_____	_____		
_____	_____		
_____	_____		
_____	_____		

Food for Thought

_____

_____

_____

Date:

Training	Time/Distance	Sets	Reps

Food for Thought

Date:

Training	Time/Distance	Sets	Reps

Food for Thought

Date:

Training	Time/Distance	Sets	Reps

Food for Thought

Date:

Training	Time/Distance	Sets	Reps

Food for Thought

Date:

Training	Time/Distance	Sets	Reps

Food for Thought

Date:

Training	Time/Distance	Sets	Reps

Food for Thought

Date:

Training	Time/Distance	Sets	Reps

Food for Thought

Date:

Training	Time/Distance	Sets	Reps

Food for Thought

Workout Wrap-Up

Accomplishments!   Notes

"The longer I run the course the closer I get to home."
— *"Preacher" Bob AuBuchon*

Training Goals

Goals!

_____

_____

_____

_____

_____

....

Date: [   ]

Training	Time/Distance	Sets	Reps
_____	_____		
_____	_____		
_____	_____		
_____	_____		
_____	_____		

Food for Thought

_____

_____

_____

....

Date: [   ]

Training	Time/Distance	Sets	Reps
_____	_____		
_____	_____		
_____	_____		
_____	_____		
_____	_____		

Food for Thought

_____

_____

_____

Date:

Training	Time/Distance	Sets	Reps

Food for Thought

_____
_____
_____

Date:

Training	Time/Distance	Sets	Reps

Food for Thought

_____
_____
_____

Date:

Training	Time/Distance	Sets	Reps

Food for Thought

_____
_____
_____

Date:

Training	Time/Distance	Sets	Reps

Food for Thought

....

Date:

Training	Time/Distance	Sets	Reps

Food for Thought

....

Date:

Training	Time/Distance	Sets	Reps

Food for Thought

Date:

Training	Time/Distance	Sets	Reps

Food for Thought

_____

_____

_____

Date:

Training	Time/Distance	Sets	Reps

Food for Thought

_____

_____

_____

Workout Wrap-Up

Accomplishments!	Notes

"I believe that every human has a finite number of heartbeats. I don't intend to waste any of mine running around doing exercises."
    — *Neil Armstrong, retired astronaut, first man on the moon*

Training Goals

Goals!

_____

_____

_____

_____

_____

. . . .

Date:

Training	Time/Distance	Sets	Reps

Food for Thought

_____

_____

_____

. . . .

Date:

Training	Time/Distance	Sets	Reps

Food for Thought

_____

_____

_____

Date:

Training	Time/Distance	Sets	Reps

_____

_____

_____

_____

_____

Food for Thought

_____

_____

_____

Date:

Training	Time/Distance	Sets	Reps

_____

_____

_____

_____

_____

Food for Thought

_____

_____

_____

Date:

Training	Time/Distance	Sets	Reps

_____

_____

_____

_____

_____

Food for Thought

_____

_____

_____

Date:

Training	Time/Distance	Sets	Reps

Food for Thought

Date:

Training	Time/Distance	Sets	Reps

Food for Thought

Date:

Training	Time/Distance	Sets	Reps

Food for Thought

Date:

Training	Time/Distance	Sets	Reps

Food for Thought

....

Date:

Training	Time/Distance	Sets	Reps

Food for Thought

Workout Wrap-Up

Accomplishments!	Notes

Training Goals

Goals!

_____
_____
_____
_____
_____

....

Date: [   ]

Training	Time/Distance	Sets	Reps

Food for Thought

_____
_____
_____

....

Date: [   ]

Training	Time/Distance	Sets	Reps

Food for Thought

_____
_____
_____

Date:

Training   Time/Distance   Sets   Reps

_____

_____

_____

_____

_____

Food for Thought

_____

_____

_____

Date:

Training   Time/Distance   Sets   Reps

_____

_____

_____

_____

_____

Food for Thought

_____

_____

_____

Date:

Training   Time/Distance   Sets   Reps

_____

_____

_____

_____

_____

Food for Thought

_____

_____

_____

Date:

Training	Time/Distance	Sets	Reps

Food for Thought

Date:

Training	Time/Distance	Sets	Reps

Food for Thought

Date:

Training	Time/Distance	Sets	Reps

Food for Thought

Date:

Training	Time/Distance	Sets	Reps

Food for Thought

_____

_____

_____

Date:

Training	Time/Distance	Sets	Reps

Food for Thought

_____

_____

_____

Workout Wrap-Up

Accomplishments!	Notes

> *"Only those who risk going too far can possibly find out how far they can go."*
>
> — *T.S. Eliot, writer*

Training Goals

Goals!

_____

_____

_____

_____

_____

Date: _____

Training	Time/Distance	Sets	Reps

Food for Thought

_____

_____

_____

Date: _____

Training	Time/Distance	Sets	Reps

Food for Thought

_____

_____

_____

Date:

Training   Time/Distance   Sets   Reps
_____
_____
_____
_____
_____

Food for Thought
_____
_____
_____

Date:

Training   Time/Distance   Sets   Reps
_____
_____
_____
_____
_____

Food for Thought
_____
_____
_____

Date:

Training   Time/Distance   Sets   Reps
_____
_____
_____
_____
_____

Food for Thought
_____
_____
_____

Date:

Training	Time/Distance	Sets	Reps

Food for Thought

_____

_____

_____

Date:

Training	Time/Distance	Sets	Reps

Food for Thought

_____

_____

_____

Date:

Training	Time/Distance	Sets	Reps

Food for Thought

_____

_____

_____

Date:

Training	Time/Distance	Sets	Reps

Food for Thought

....

Date:

Training	Time/Distance	Sets	Reps

Food for Thought

Workout Wrap-Up

Accomplishments!   Notes

Training Goals

Goals!

_____
_____
_____
_____
_____

....

Date: _____

Training	Time/Distance	Sets	Reps

Food for Thought

_____
_____
_____

....

Date: _____

Training	Time/Distance	Sets	Reps

Food for Thought

_____
_____
_____

Date:

Training	Time/Distance	Sets	Reps

Food for Thought

Date:

Training	Time/Distance	Sets	Reps

Food for Thought

Date:

Training	Time/Distance	Sets	Reps

Food for Thought

Date:

Training   Time/Distance   Sets   Reps

_____

_____

_____

_____

_____

Food for Thought

_____

_____

_____

....

Date:

Training   Time/Distance   Sets   Reps

_____

_____

_____

_____

_____

Food for Thought

_____

_____

_____

....

Date:

Training   Time/Distance   Sets   Reps

_____

_____

_____

_____

_____

Food for Thought

_____

_____

_____

Date:

Training	Time/Distance	Sets	Reps

Food for Thought

....

Date:

Training	Time/Distance	Sets	Reps

Food for Thought

Workout Wrap-Up

Accomplishments!	Notes

"We're all brothers and sisters in this sport. I'll see you on the roads."

— *Bill Rodgers, Boston Marathon winner*

Training Goals

Goals!

_____
_____
_____
_____
_____

....

Date: [_____]

Training	Time/Distance	Sets	Reps
_____	_____		
_____	_____		
_____	_____		
_____	_____		
_____	_____		

Food for Thought

_____
_____
_____

....

Date: [_____]

Training	Time/Distance	Sets	Reps
_____	_____		
_____	_____		
_____	_____		
_____	_____		
_____	_____		

Food for Thought

_____
_____
_____

Date:

Training	Time/Distance	Sets	Reps

Food for Thought

Date:

Training	Time/Distance	Sets	Reps

Food for Thought

Date:

Training	Time/Distance	Sets	Reps

Food for Thought

Date:

Training	Time/Distance	Sets	Reps

Food for Thought

....

Date:

Training	Time/Distance	Sets	Reps

Food for Thought

....

Date:

Training	Time/Distance	Sets	Reps

Food for Thought

Date:

Training	Time/Distance	Sets	Reps

Food for Thought

. . . .

Date:

Training	Time/Distance	Sets	Reps

Food for Thought

Workout Wrap-Up

Accomplishments!	Notes

NO SWEAT

"Avoid running at all times. Don't look back. Something may be gaining on you."

— Leroy "Satchel" Paige, Hall of Fame pitcher

Training Goals

Goals!

_____
_____
_____
_____
_____

....

Date: _____

Training	Time/Distance	Sets	Reps
_____	_____		
_____	_____		
_____	_____		
_____	_____		
_____	_____		

Food for Thought

_____
_____
_____

....

Date: _____

Training	Time/Distance	Sets	Reps
_____	_____		
_____	_____		
_____	_____		
_____	_____		
_____	_____		

Food for Thought

_____
_____
_____

Date:

Training	Time/Distance	Sets	Reps

Food for Thought

....

Date:

Training	Time/Distance	Sets	Reps

Food for Thought

....

Date:

Training	Time/Distance	Sets	Reps

Food for Thought

Date:

Training	Time/Distance	Sets	Reps

Food for Thought

_____

_____

_____

Date:

Training	Time/Distance	Sets	Reps

Food for Thought

_____

_____

_____

Date:

Training	Time/Distance	Sets	Reps

Food for Thought

_____

_____

_____

Date:

Training	Time/Distance	Sets	Reps

Food for Thought

___

Date:

Training	Time/Distance	Sets	Reps

Food for Thought

___

Workout Wrap-Up

Accomplishments!	Notes

"He may win the race that runs by himself."
— Benjamin Franklin, writer and inventor

Training Goals

Goals!

_____

_____

_____

_____

_____

. . . .

Date:

Training	Time/Distance	Sets	Reps

Food for Thought

_____

_____

_____

. . . .

Date:

Training	Time/Distance	Sets	Reps

Food for Thought

_____

_____

_____

Date:

Training	Time/Distance	Sets	Reps

Food for Thought

Date:

Training	Time/Distance	Sets	Reps

Food for Thought

Date:

Training	Time/Distance	Sets	Reps

Food for Thought

Date:

Training	Time/Distance	Sets	Reps

Food for Thought

....

Date:

Training	Time/Distance	Sets	Reps

Food for Thought

....

Date:

Training	Time/Distance	Sets	Reps

Food for Thought

Date:

Training	Time/Distance	Sets	Reps

Food for Thought

....

Date:

Training	Time/Distance	Sets	Reps

Food for Thought

Workout Wrap-Up

Accomplishments!	Notes

"There is a time to run and there is a time to rest. It is the true test of the runner to get them both right."
— Noel Carroll, Irish Olympian

Training Goals

Goals!

_____
_____
_____
_____
_____

Date: [   ]

Training	Time/Distance	Sets	Reps

Food for Thought

_____
_____
_____

Date: [   ]

Training	Time/Distance	Sets	Reps

Food for Thought

_____
_____
_____

Date:

Training	Time/Distance	Sets	Reps

Food for Thought

. . . .

Date:

Training	Time/Distance	Sets	Reps

Food for Thought

. . . .

Date:

Training	Time/Distance	Sets	Reps

Food for Thought

Date:

Training	Time/Distance	Sets	Reps

Food for Thought

Date:

Training	Time/Distance	Sets	Reps

Food for Thought

Date:

Training	Time/Distance	Sets	Reps

Food for Thought

Date:

Training	Time/Distance	Sets	Reps

Food for Thought

Date:

Training	Time/Distance	Sets	Reps

Food for Thought

Workout Wrap-Up

Accomplishments!	Notes

"If I'd known I was gonna live this long, I'd have taken better care of myself."

— Eubie Blake, jazz pianist, at age 100

Training Goals

Goals!

_____

_____

_____

_____

_____

. . . .

Date: _____

Training	Time/Distance	Sets	Reps

Food for Thought

_____

_____

_____

. . . .

Date: _____

Training	Time/Distance	Sets	Reps

Food for Thought

_____

_____

_____

Date:

Training	Time/Distance	Sets	Reps

Food for Thought

Date:

Training	Time/Distance	Sets	Reps

Food for Thought

Date:

Training	Time/Distance	Sets	Reps

Food for Thought

Date:

Training   Time/Distance   Sets   Reps

_____

_____

_____

_____

_____

Food for Thought

_____

_____

_____

Date:

Training   Time/Distance   Sets   Reps

_____

_____

_____

_____

_____

Food for Thought

_____

_____

_____

Date:

Training   Time/Distance   Sets   Reps

_____

_____

_____

_____

_____

Food for Thought

_____

_____

_____

Date:

Training	Time/Distance	Sets	Reps

Food for Thought

Date:

Training	Time/Distance	Sets	Reps

Food for Thought

Workout Wrap-Up

Accomplishments!   Notes

"If a man coaches himself, then he has only himself to blame when he is beaten."
— Roger Bannister, first man to break the four-minute mile

Training Goals

Goals!

_____

_____

_____

_____

_____

....

Date: _____

Training	Time/Distance	Sets	Reps

Food for Thought

_____

_____

_____

....

Date: _____

Training	Time/Distance	Sets	Reps

Food for Thought

_____

_____

_____

Date:

Training   Time/Distance   Sets   Reps

_____

_____

_____

_____

Food for Thought

_____

_____

_____

Date:

Training   Time/Distance   Sets   Reps

_____

_____

_____

_____

Food for Thought

_____

_____

_____

Date:

Training   Time/Distance   Sets   Reps

_____

_____

_____

_____

Food for Thought

_____

_____

_____

Date:

Training	Time/Distance	Sets	Reps

Food for Thought

Date:

Training	Time/Distance	Sets	Reps

Food for Thought

Date:

Training	Time/Distance	Sets	Reps

Food for Thought

Date:

Training	Time/Distance	Sets	Reps

Food for Thought

Date:

Training	Time/Distance	Sets	Reps

Food for Thought

Workout Wrap-Up

Accomplishments!	Notes

"I cannot believe that our muscular vigor will ever be a super-fluity. Even if the day ever dawns in which it will not be needed for fighting the old heavy battles against Nature, it will always be needed to furnish the background of sanity, serenity and cheerfulness to life, to give moral elasticity to our disposition, to round off the wiry edge of our fretfulness, and make us good humored and easy of approach."

— *William James, American philosopher*

Training Goals

Goals!

_____

_____

_____

Date: _____

Training	Time/Distance	Sets	Reps
_____	_____		
_____	_____		
_____	_____		
_____	_____		
_____	_____		

Food for Thought

_____

_____

_____

Date: _____

Training	Time/Distance	Sets	Reps
_____	_____		
_____	_____		
_____	_____		
_____	_____		
_____	_____		

Food for Thought

_____

_____

_____

Date:

Training	Time/Distance	Sets	Reps

Food for Thought

Date:

Training	Time/Distance	Sets	Reps

Food for Thought

Date:

Training	Time/Distance	Sets	Reps

Food for Thought

Date:

Training	Time/Distance	Sets	Reps

Food for Thought

Date:

Training	Time/Distance	Sets	Reps

Food for Thought

Date:

Training	Time/Distance	Sets	Reps

Food for Thought

Date:

Training	Time/Distance	Sets	Reps

Food for Thought

....

Date:

Training	Time/Distance	Sets	Reps

Food for Thought

Workout Wrap-Up

Accomplishments!	Notes

"I wanted the world to know that my country Ethiopia has always won with determination and heroism."
— Abebe Bikila, after winning the 1960 Olympic marathon barefoot

Training Goals

Goals!

_____
_____
_____
_____
_____

. . . .

Date: [   ]

Training	Time/Distance	Sets	Reps
_____	_____		
_____	_____		
_____	_____		
_____	_____		
_____	_____		

Food for Thought

_____
_____
_____

. . . .

Date: [   ]

Training	Time/Distance	Sets	Reps
_____	_____		
_____	_____		
_____	_____		
_____	_____		
_____	_____		

Food for Thought

_____
_____
_____

Date:

Training	Time/Distance	Sets	Reps

Food for Thought

Date:

Training	Time/Distance	Sets	Reps

Food for Thought

Date:

Training	Time/Distance	Sets	Reps

Food for Thought

Date:

Training	Time/Distance	Sets	Reps

Food for Thought

Date:

Training	Time/Distance	Sets	Reps

Food for Thought

Date:

Training	Time/Distance	Sets	Reps

Food for Thought

Date:

Training	Time/Distance	Sets	Reps

Food for Thought

Date:

Training	Time/Distance	Sets	Reps

Food for Thought

Workout Wrap-Up

Accomplishments! | Notes

NO SWEAT

"Exercise is bunk. If you are healthy, you don't need it; if you are sick, you shouldn't take it."

— Henry Ford

Training Goals

Goals!

_____
_____
_____
_____
_____

....

Date: [_____]

Training	Time/Distance	Sets	Reps
_____	_____		
_____	_____		
_____	_____		
_____	_____		
_____	_____		

Food for Thought

_____
_____
_____

....

Date: [_____]

Training	Time/Distance	Sets	Reps
_____	_____		
_____	_____		
_____	_____		
_____	_____		
_____	_____		

Food for Thought

_____
_____
_____

Date:

Training   Time/Distance   Sets   Reps

_____

_____

_____

_____

_____

Food for Thought

_____

_____

_____

Date:

Training   Time/Distance   Sets   Reps

_____

_____

_____

_____

_____

Food for Thought

_____

_____

_____

Date:

Training   Time/Distance   Sets   Reps

_____

_____

_____

_____

_____

Food for Thought

_____

_____

_____

Date:

Training   Time/Distance   Sets   Reps

_____

_____

_____

_____

_____

Food for Thought

_____

_____

_____

Date:

Training   Time/Distance   Sets   Reps

_____

_____

_____

_____

_____

Food for Thought

_____

_____

_____

Date:

Training   Time/Distance   Sets   Reps

_____

_____

_____

_____

_____

Food for Thought

_____

_____

_____

Date:

Training	Time/Distance	Sets	Reps

Food for Thought

_____

_____

_____

Date:

Training	Time/Distance	Sets	Reps

Food for Thought

_____

_____

_____

Workout Wrap-Up

Accomplishments!	Notes

"Take care of your body with steadfast fidelity. The soul must see through these eyes alone, and if they are dim, the whole world is clouded."

— *J.W. Goethe, poet and dramatist*

Training Goals

Goals!

_____

_____

_____

_____

_____

....

Date:

Training	Time/Distance	Sets	Reps
_____	_____		
_____	_____		
_____	_____		
_____	_____		
_____	_____		

Food for Thought

_____

_____

_____

....

Date:

Training	Time/Distance	Sets	Reps
_____	_____		
_____	_____		
_____	_____		
_____	_____		
_____	_____		

Food for Thought

_____

_____

_____

Date:

Training	Time/Distance	Sets	Reps

Food for Thought

Date:

Training	Time/Distance	Sets	Reps

Food for Thought

Date:

Training	Time/Distance	Sets	Reps

Food for Thought

Date:

Training	Time/Distance	Sets	Reps

Food for Thought

Date:

Training	Time/Distance	Sets	Reps

Food for Thought

Date:

Training	Time/Distance	Sets	Reps

Food for Thought

Date:

Training   Time/Distance   Sets   Reps

Food for Thought

....

Date:

Training   Time/Distance   Sets   Reps

Food for Thought

Workout Wrap-Up

Accomplishments!   Notes

Training Goals

Goals!

_____

_____

_____

_____

_____

....

Date: _____

Training	Time/Distance	Sets	Reps

Food for Thought

_____

_____

_____

....

Date: _____

Training	Time/Distance	Sets	Reps

Food for Thought

_____

_____

_____

Date:

Training	Time/Distance	Sets	Reps

Food for Thought

....

Date:

Training	Time/Distance	Sets	Reps

Food for Thought

....

Date:

Training	Time/Distance	Sets	Reps

Food for Thought

Date:

Training	Time/Distance	Sets	Reps

Food for Thought

....

Date:

Training	Time/Distance	Sets	Reps

Food for Thought

....

Date:

Training	Time/Distance	Sets	Reps

Food for Thought

Date:

Training	Time/Distance	Sets	Reps

Food for Thought

_____

_____

_____

Date:

Training	Time/Distance	Sets	Reps

Food for Thought

_____

_____

_____

Workout Wrap-Up

Accomplishments!	Notes

"Why should I learn to practice running slow? I already now how to run slow. I must learn how to run fast."
— Emil Zatopek, Olympic Marathon champion

Training Goals

Goals!

_____
_____
_____
_____
_____

....

Date:

Training	Time/Distance	Sets	Reps

Food for Thought

_____
_____
_____

....

Date:

Training	Time/Distance	Sets	Reps

Food for Thought

_____
_____
_____

Date:

Training   Time/Distance   Sets   Reps

Food for Thought

Date:

Training   Time/Distance   Sets   Reps

Food for Thought

Date:

Training   Time/Distance   Sets   Reps

Food for Thought

Date:

Training	Time/Distance	Sets	Reps

Food for Thought

Date:

Training	Time/Distance	Sets	Reps

Food for Thought

Date:

Training	Time/Distance	Sets	Reps

Food for Thought

Date:

Training	Time/Distance	Sets	Reps

Food for Thought

_____

_____

_____

Date:

Training	Time/Distance	Sets	Reps

Food for Thought

_____

_____

_____

Workout Wrap-Up

Accomplishments!	Notes

Training Goals

Goals!

_____

_____

_____

_____

_____

....

Date: _____

Training	Time/Distance	Sets	Reps
_____	_____		
_____	_____		
_____	_____		
_____	_____		
_____	_____		

Food for Thought

_____

_____

_____

....

Date: _____

Training	Time/Distance	Sets	Reps
_____	_____		
_____	_____		
_____	_____		
_____	_____		
_____	_____		

Food for Thought

_____

_____

_____

Date:

Training	Time/Distance	Sets	Reps

Food for Thought

....

Date:

Training	Time/Distance	Sets	Reps

Food for Thought

....

Date:

Training	Time/Distance	Sets	Reps

Food for Thought

Date:

Training   Time/Distance   Sets   Reps

_____

_____

_____

_____

_____

Food for Thought

_____

_____

_____

....

Date:

Training   Time/Distance   Sets   Reps

_____

_____

_____

_____

_____

Food for Thought

_____

_____

_____

....

Date:

Training   Time/Distance   Sets   Reps

_____

_____

_____

_____

_____

Food for Thought

_____

_____

_____

Date:

Training	Time/Distance	Sets	Reps

Food for Thought

Date:

Training	Time/Distance	Sets	Reps

Food for Thought

Workout Wrap-Up

Accomplishments!	Notes

"The secret of health for both mind and body is not to mourn for the past, not to worry about the future, or not to anticipate troubles, but to live the present moment wisely and earnestly."
— *Buddha, the Enlightened One*

Training Goals

Goals!

_____
_____
_____
_____
_____

Date: _____

Training	Time/Distance	Sets	Reps
_____	_____		
_____	_____		
_____	_____		
_____	_____		
_____	_____		

Food for Thought

_____
_____
_____

Date: _____

Training	Time/Distance	Sets	Reps
_____	_____		
_____	_____		
_____	_____		
_____	_____		
_____	_____		

Food for Thought

_____
_____
_____

Date:

Training   Time/Distance   Sets   Reps

_____

_____

_____

_____

_____

Food for Thought

_____

_____

_____

Date:

Training   Time/Distance   Sets   Reps

_____

_____

_____

_____

_____

Food for Thought

_____

_____

_____

Date:

Training   Time/Distance   Sets   Reps

_____

_____

_____

_____

_____

Food for Thought

_____

_____

_____

Date:

Training   Time/Distance   Sets   Reps

_____

_____

_____

_____

_____

Food for Thought

_____

_____

_____

....

Date:

Training   Time/Distance   Sets   Reps

_____

_____

_____

_____

_____

Food for Thought

_____

_____

_____

....

Date:

Training   Time/Distance   Sets   Reps

_____

_____

_____

_____

_____

Food for Thought

_____

_____

_____

Date:

Training	Time/Distance	Sets	Reps

Food for Thought

....

Date:

Training	Time/Distance	Sets	Reps

Food for Thought

Workout Wrap-Up

Accomplishments!	Notes

"For me, the real joy of running and racing is finding out what I am capable of on any given day. I start every race with my actual watch and my emotional watch set to 00:00. I try to stand at every starting line filled not with dread, but with curiosity. And I cross every finish line with a sense of reverence and satisfaction."
— John "The Penguin" Bingham, Runner's World *columnist*

Training Goals

Goals!

_____
_____
_____
_____
_____

....

Date:

Training	Time/Distance	Sets	Reps

Food for Thought

_____
_____
_____

....

Date:

Training	Time/Distance	Sets	Reps

Food for Thought

_____
_____
_____

Date:

Training	Time/Distance	Sets	Reps

Food for Thought

Date:

Training	Time/Distance	Sets	Reps

Food for Thought

Date:

Training	Time/Distance	Sets	Reps

Food for Thought

Date:

Training	Time/Distance	Sets	Reps

Food for Thought

....

Date:

Training	Time/Distance	Sets	Reps

Food for Thought

....

Date:

Training	Time/Distance	Sets	Reps

Food for Thought

Date: _____

Training   Time/Distance   Sets   Reps

_____   [ ]   [ ]
_____   [ ]   [ ]
_____   [ ]   [ ]
_____   [ ]   [ ]
_____   [ ]   [ ]

Food for Thought

_____
_____
_____

....

Date: _____

Training   Time/Distance   Sets   Reps

_____   [ ]   [ ]
_____   [ ]   [ ]
_____   [ ]   [ ]
_____   [ ]   [ ]
_____   [ ]   [ ]

Food for Thought

_____
_____
_____

Workout Wrap-Up

Accomplishments!   Notes

_____   _____
_____   _____
_____   _____
_____   _____
_____   _____
_____   _____
_____   _____

Training Goals

Goals!

....

Date:

Training	Time/Distance	Sets	Reps

Food for Thought

....

Date:

Training	Time/Distance	Sets	Reps

Food for Thought

Date:

Training   Time/Distance   Sets   Reps

_____

_____

_____

_____

_____

Food for Thought

_____

_____

_____

Date:

Training   Time/Distance   Sets   Reps

_____

_____

_____

_____

_____

Food for Thought

_____

_____

_____

Date:

Training   Time/Distance   Sets   Reps

_____

_____

_____

_____

_____

Food for Thought

_____

_____

_____

Date:

Training	Time/Distance	Sets	Reps

Food for Thought

Date:

Training	Time/Distance	Sets	Reps

Food for Thought

Date:

Training	Time/Distance	Sets	Reps

Food for Thought

Date:

Training   Time/Distance   Sets   Reps

_____

_____

_____

_____

_____

Food for Thought

_____

_____

_____

Date:

Training   Time/Distance   Sets   Reps

_____

_____

_____

_____

_____

Food for Thought

_____

_____

_____

Workout Wrap-Up

Accomplishments!   Notes

_____   _____

_____   _____

_____   _____

_____   _____

_____   _____

_____   _____

"People say I've given people courage. That makes me feel good, but I don't see how I do that. I think my running is a self-ish thing. But it provides the challenge that allows me to feel good about myself. How can I expect to do well in other activities if I don't feel good about myself?"
— Joan Benoit, Olympic Marathon champion

Training Goals

Goals!

_____
_____
_____
_____
_____

Date:

Training	Time/Distance	Sets	Reps

Food for Thought

_____
_____
_____

Date:

Training	Time/Distance	Sets	Reps

Food for Thought

_____
_____
_____

Date:

Training	Time/Distance	Sets	Reps

Food for Thought

Date:

Training	Time/Distance	Sets	Reps

Food for Thought

Date:

Training	Time/Distance	Sets	Reps

Food for Thought

Date:

Training	Time/Distance	Sets	Reps

Food for Thought

Date:

Training	Time/Distance	Sets	Reps

Food for Thought

Date:

Training	Time/Distance	Sets	Reps

Food for Thought

Date:

Training   Time/Distance   Sets   Reps

_____

_____

_____

_____

_____

Food for Thought

_____

_____

_____

Date:

Training   Time/Distance   Sets   Reps

_____

_____

_____

_____

_____

Food for Thought

_____

_____

_____

Workout Wrap-Up

Accomplishments!   Notes

_____   _____

_____   _____

_____   _____

_____   _____

_____   _____

_____   _____

_____   _____

"A pint of sweat saves a gallon of blood."
— George Patton, U.S. Army General

Training Goals

Goals!

....

Date:

Training	Time/Distance	Sets	Reps

Food for Thought

....

Date:

Training	Time/Distance	Sets	Reps

Food for Thought

Date:

Training   Time/Distance   Sets   Reps

_____
_____
_____
_____
_____

Food for Thought

_____
_____
_____

Date:

Training   Time/Distance   Sets   Reps

_____
_____
_____
_____
_____

Food for Thought

_____
_____
_____

Date:

Training   Time/Distance   Sets   Reps

_____
_____
_____
_____
_____

Food for Thought

_____
_____
_____

Date:

Training   Time/Distance   Sets   Reps

_____

_____

_____

_____

_____

Food for Thought

_____

_____

_____

....

Date:

Training   Time/Distance   Sets   Reps

_____

_____

_____

_____

_____

Food for Thought

_____

_____

_____

....

Date:

Training   Time/Distance   Sets   Reps

_____

_____

_____

_____

_____

Food for Thought

_____

_____

_____

Date:

Training	Time/Distance	Sets	Reps

Food for Thought

Date:

Training	Time/Distance	Sets	Reps

Food for Thought

Workout Wrap-Up

Accomplishments!   Notes

"Slow running just makes you a slow runner."
— *Grete Waitz, nine-time winner of the*
New York City Marathon

Training Goals
Goals!

_____

_____

_____

_____

_____

· ·

Date:

Training	Time/Distance	Sets	Reps

Food for Thought

_____

_____

_____

· ·

Date:

Training	Time/Distance	Sets	Reps

Food for Thought

_____

_____

_____

Date:

Training	Time/Distance	Sets	Reps

Food for Thought

Date:

Training	Time/Distance	Sets	Reps

Food for Thought

Date:

Training	Time/Distance	Sets	Reps

Food for Thought

Date:

Training   Time/Distance   Sets   Reps

_____

_____

_____

_____

_____

Food for Thought

_____

_____

_____

Date:

Training   Time/Distance   Sets   Reps

_____

_____

_____

_____

_____

Food for Thought

_____

_____

_____

Date:

Training   Time/Distance   Sets   Reps

_____

_____

_____

_____

_____

Food for Thought

_____

_____

_____

Date:

Training	Time/Distance	Sets	Reps

Food for Thought

....

Date:

Training	Time/Distance	Sets	Reps

Food for Thought

Workout Wrap-Up

Accomplishments!   Notes

"Now my task is smoothly done/I can fly or I can run."
— John Milton, writer

Training Goals

Goals!

_____
_____
_____
_____
_____

Date: _____

Training	Time/Distance	Sets	Reps

Food for Thought

_____
_____
_____

Date: _____

Training	Time/Distance	Sets	Reps

Food for Thought

_____
_____
_____

Date:

Training   Time/Distance   Sets   Reps

_____

_____

_____

_____

_____

Food for Thought

_____

_____

_____

Date:

Training   Time/Distance   Sets   Reps

_____

_____

_____

_____

_____

Food for Thought

_____

_____

_____

Date:

Training   Time/Distance   Sets   Reps

_____

_____

_____

_____

_____

Food for Thought

_____

_____

_____

Date:

Training	Time/Distance	Sets	Reps

Food for Thought

Date:

Training	Time/Distance	Sets	Reps

Food for Thought

Date:

Training	Time/Distance	Sets	Reps

Food for Thought

Date:

Training	Time/Distance	Sets	Reps

Food for Thought

....

Date:

Training	Time/Distance	Sets	Reps

Food for Thought

Workout Wrap-Up

Accomplishments!   Notes

"In anguish we uplift/A new unhallowed song/The race is to the swift/The battle to the strong"
— *John Davidson, singer and game show host*

Training Goals

Goals!

_____
_____
_____
_____
_____

Date: _____

Training	Time/Distance	Sets	Reps
_____	_____		
_____	_____		
_____	_____		
_____	_____		
_____	_____		

Food for Thought
_____
_____
_____

Date: _____

Training	Time/Distance	Sets	Reps
_____	_____		
_____	_____		
_____	_____		
_____	_____		
_____	_____		

Food for Thought
_____
_____
_____

Date:

Training   Time/Distance   Sets   Reps

_____

_____

_____

_____

_____

Food for Thought

_____

_____

_____

Date:

Training   Time/Distance   Sets   Reps

_____

_____

_____

_____

_____

Food for Thought

_____

_____

_____

Date:

Training   Time/Distance   Sets   Reps

_____

_____

_____

_____

_____

Food for Thought

_____

_____

_____

Date:

Training — Time/Distance — Sets — Reps

_____

_____

_____

_____

_____

Food for Thought

_____

_____

_____

Date:

Training — Time/Distance — Sets — Reps

_____

_____

_____

_____

_____

Food for Thought

_____

_____

_____

Date:

Training — Time/Distance — Sets — Reps

_____

_____

_____

_____

_____

Food for Thought

_____

_____

_____

Date:

Training	Time/Distance	Sets	Reps

Food for Thought

Date:

Training	Time/Distance	Sets	Reps

Food for Thought

Workout Wrap-Up

Accomplishments!   Notes

"I like long walks, especially when they are taken by people who annoy me."

— Fred Allen, comedian

Training Goals

Goals!

_____
_____
_____
_____
_____

....

Date: [   ]

Training	Time/Distance	Sets	Reps

Food for Thought
_____
_____
_____

....

Date: [   ]

Training	Time/Distance	Sets	Reps

Food for Thought
_____
_____
_____

Date:

Training	Time/Distance	Sets	Reps

Food for Thought

Date:

Training	Time/Distance	Sets	Reps

Food for Thought

Date:

Training	Time/Distance	Sets	Reps

Food for Thought

Date:

Training	Time/Distance	Sets	Reps

Food for Thought

_____

_____

_____

....

Date:

Training	Time/Distance	Sets	Reps

Food for Thought

_____

_____

_____

....

Date:

Training	Time/Distance	Sets	Reps

Food for Thought

_____

_____

_____

Date:

Training	Time/Distance	Sets	Reps

Food for Thought

....

Date:

Training	Time/Distance	Sets	Reps

Food for Thought

Workout Wrap-Up

Accomplishments!	Notes

Part III
The Part of Tens

The 5th Wave   By Rich Tennant

"You know, anyone who wishes he had a remote control for his exercise equipment is missing the idea of exercise equipment."

In this part . . .

*E*veryone loves a list, right? Well, the Part of Tens pages are like dessert, a few quick tips to help make exercising something that's not only good for you, but fun, too. Think of it as spinach salad with a crème brûlée chaser.

Chapter 5

Ten Top Race Essentials

The cool thing about running is that you don't need a lot of gear. But if you get to the starting line without any of these things, you may be sorry later.

Sunglasses

Not only will your eyes thank you for sunglasses — they'll fight glare and debris — a good pair will also help hide the grimace during your more difficult moments. In other words, they help you both see and look better.

Sunscreen

You face enough physical challenges without a sunburn. But remember to wear sports-specific screen, which won't sweat off, and more importantly, won't drip into your eyes and have you squinting through the last four miles.

Cash

As a guy on a train in Scotland once said to me "You can't have any fun, if you don't have any mon. . . ." We assume he meant money, and without some, you're not going to be able to buy a post-race snack or even a cab ride back home.

A Quarter

Or 35 cents or whatever your local phone company deems a reasonable fee for the use of a public phone. You never know when you'll need it.

Some ID

Bring along a small card that has your address, a phone number, your health insurance numbers, and emergency contact numbers. In fact, it's not a bad idea for training runs too.

A Watch

Sure, that big clock at the finish will tell you how fast you ran. But your watch will give you intermediate splits that'll make sure that your crossing-the-tape time will be a personal record.

Spare Shoelaces

Murphy's Law being what it is, those shoelaces that have served you admirably for six months will snap in half as soon as you step up to the line. So bring a spare pair. It beats securing your shoe with duct tape.

Your Race Number

What could be worse than getting to the finish line, only to have the persons holding the tape shake their head? Your time doesn't count if you don't have a number. And don't forget safety pins to attach it.

Food

A runner doesn't run on willpower alone. So make sure you've packed energy bars, sports gel, or some low-tech fuel like a banana and a few fig bars for a quick energy boost before the race, or for quick refueling. The choice is yours, but you want something easily digested.

Whatever Makes You Happy (For When You Reach the Finish Line)

Is it your lucky baseball cap, your mini-radio, a stuffed animal, a bottle of Ibuprofen? And don't forget personal necessities, like contact lenses and prescription medications.

Chapter 6

Ten Top Running Songs

In This Chapter

▶ Nowhere to hide . . . (from training)

▶ I ran, ran so far away . . .

▶ I don't feel so bad now . . .

*O*ne of the best ways to hit your stride is by playing great music. Here are ten songs that will provide a soundtrack to even your longest runs.

"Nowhere to Run," Martha Reeves and the Vandellas

This Motown anthem of obsessive love is one of the great all-but-forgotten classics by the greatest all-but-forgotten girl group.

"Born to Run," Bruce Springsteen

Rock critic Greil Marcus said that this Spector-influenced anthem sounds "like a '57 Chevy running on melted down Crystals's records."

"Running on Empty," Jackson Browne

A classic soft-rock reminder to eat right and drink plenty of fluids. All set to a beat you can dance to. Sorta.

"Runaway," Del Shannon

Forget the first line "As I walk along" and get into the driving minor chord beat and Shannon's achingly defiant vocal. Bonnie Raitt does a fine version, too.

"Band on the Run," Paul McCartney

Yeah, it's fluff, but nobody does fluff better than the Beatles' popmeister.

"Runaround," Blues Traveler

Pop in this piece of perfect John Popper-powered pop at the end of a workout, and you'll be tempted to add on an extra mile.

"Roadrunner," Modern Lovers

Jonathan Richman's two-chord paean to the joys of suburbia was an inspiration to the punks and new wavers who realized you didn't have to have Jimi Hendrix chops to write a great rock song.

"Running on Faith," Eric Clapton

A product of the dark days after his son's death, this ballad has a quiet strength that lies beneath its adult-contemporary surface.

"Long May You Run," Neil Young

Listen carefully, and you'll realize that this mournful ballad is an ode to a gone-but-not forgotten pickup truck. And the human-powered journey home.

"Walk Don't Run," The Ventures

This seminal surf music instrumental might just convince you to do a little cross-training — at the Bansai Pipeline.

Index

Notes

Notes

Notes